13 PRINCIPLES OF EMUNA

The Timeless Foundations of Jewish Faith

By Rabbi Lazer Brody

Author of:

Three Words of Emuna
The Worry Worm
The Path to Your Peak
Old Isaac's Trail to Tranquility
Chassidic Pearls
And other titles

An Emuna Beams Publication

Acknowledgements

The Gemara says two of the three partners who bring a person into the world are one's parents. I therefore dedicate this book to the beloved memories of my mother and father, Chasia bas Gamliel Halevi ob"m and Yaacov ben Yitzchak, ob"m. May their cherished souls bask in eternal Divine light and may all their offspring follow the path of Torah and emuna, amen.

There's a third partner in bringing a person to the world – the Almighty, my beloved Father in Heaven, Who has protected and sustained me always and accorded me the privilege of writing this book and helping to make people's lives a little bit happier.

My spiritual guide and teacher – the honorable Grand Rabbi Naftali Asher Yishayahu Moshkovitz shlit'a, aka the "Melitzer Rebbe of Ashdod", son after son of the holy Rebbe Michel'e of Zlatshov osb"m, took me under his wing nearly three decades ago, teaching me the ABC's of Torah outlook and pure Divine service, while becoming my shining role model of what a scholarly, humble and upright spiritual guide should be. May the Almighty grant the Rebbe shlit'a longevity, good health and gratification from his students and offspring.

My cherished wife Yehudit, my unequivocal best friend and lifelong partner, has forever been a woman of valor standing faithfully at my side. She deserves the credit not only for this project, but for every other blessing in my life. To her happiness and good health, I also dedicate this book.

Mrs. Yehudit Bell deserves a special bouquet of gratitude for her tireless editing and proofing contributions to this book. May she and her family enjoy everything good in material and spiritual abundance always.

May we soon see the day when the entire world fills with the knowledge of Hashem and all of humanity calls out His Name, amen!

Lazer Brody

Approbation

Grand Rabbi N. Moskowitz
The Melitzer Rebbe of Ashdod

Cheshvan, 5781

My distinguished friend, provider of merit to the masses Rabbi Eliezer Raphoel ("Lazer") Brody shlit'a whom I know very well has come to me, and he is a G-d fearing Torah scholar who serves Hashem with all his might, and for many years already has been teaching and lecturing on the lofty subject of *emuna* (faith) in the Almighty, which is the foundation of Judaism, but because of rote habit and life's challenges, this subject has been forgotten, and it eludes people's hearts. This is apparent in all areas of life, whether between man and G-d or between man and fellow human. It is the author's tremendous privilege to traverse the globe, to publicize and to reinforce the belief in G-d in people's hearts, and many have mended their ways and changed their lives for the better by virtue of his words that come from the heart. Now, he has shown me his book "**13 Principles of Emuna**", which shows how people can build their solid faith in the Creator, blessed be His Name. It is befitting to read, learn and internalize the meaningful and encouraging concepts presented in this book, which surely will bring readers benefit both in material and spiritual areas.

I bless the distinguished author that he may continue and expand his activities in inspiring the masses to strengthen their faith in G-d and may he succeed in all his endeavors.

And on all this, I hereby sign,

Naftali Moskowitz

Table of Contents

13 Principles of Emuna: An Overview

The monumental 12th Century CE teacher, scholar and codifier of Jewish Law Rabbi Moshe ben Maimon ("Maimonides" also known as "The Rambam"), gleaned all of Torah and compiled thirteen essential principles of faith, what we refer to throughout this book as the "Thirteen Principles of Emuna," the fundamental truths of our belief in God[1]. They are as follows:

Principle 1: I believe with complete belief that the Creator, blessed be His Name, is Creator and Director of all the

---

[1] Throughout this book, we also refer to God as "the Almighty", "the Creator" or simply "Hashem", which in Hebrew means "The Name," a term frequently used to avoid speaking or writing the Divine Name unnecessarily, outside the context of prayer and benedictions.

creations, and He alone did, does and will do every deed.

This is the belief in the existence of the Creator and that He is the life force behind all of creation; nothing can exist without His will, from the mega-galaxies to the tiniest parts of an atom. The Creator makes everything happen and nothing can happen or exist against His will. "There is no one but Him" (Deuteronomy 4:35).

Principle 2: I believe with complete belief that the Creator blessed be His Name is One and there is no unity like Him under any circumstances and He alone is our God, past, present and future.

This is the belief that the Creator is the One and only God, Who is a perfect inseparable unified whole with no co-deities whatsoever, independent of everyone and everything, as we say in the *Shema* prayer, "Here O Israel, the Lord our God, the Lord is One" (Deuteronomy 6:4).

Principle 3: I believe with complete belief that the Creator blessed be His Name is not a body, nor can any

physical entity comprehend Him. He is incorporeal, with no image whatsoever.

The Creator defies any description, nor can a mortal understand Him or His workings in any way. Kabbalistic terminology refers to Hashem as *Ein Sof*, "The Infinite", for there is nothing tangible or finite about Hashem.

Principle 4: I believe with complete belief that the Creator blessed be His Name is first and last.

This is the belief that Creator defies time and space. He is infinite and eternal, preceding the beginning of time, existing forever even after the end of time.

Principle 5: I believe with complete belief that the Creator blessed be His Name is the only entity to whom it is befitting to pray, and it is not befitting to pray to anyone or anything else.

This is the foundation of monotheism, forbidding idolatry and false gods, thereby precluding worship or submission to anyone or anything else other than the Creator.

Principle 6: I believe with complete belief that all the words of the prophets are true.

We believe in the prophecies of all the forty-eight prophets and seven prophetesses mentioned in the *Tanach* and do not doubt that their prophecies are the word of Hashem and therefore truth.

Principle 7: I believe with complete belief that the prophecy of Moses, may he rest in peace, was real, and that he was the foremost of the all the prophets, the ones before him and the ones after him.

We believe that the "Five Books of Moses" – the Torah – was given to Moses from Hashem and that every word is absolute truth. Whereas prophecy was Hashem's way of speaking to the prophets, we believe that Hashem spoke to Moses directly (Exodus 33:11, Deuteronomy 34:10).

Principle 8: I believe with complete belief that the entire Torah we have in

our possession today is the one given to Moses, may he rest in peace.

This is the belief in the Divine origin of our Torah, for the Torah we read and learn today is the exact same Torah that Hashem gave to Moses.

Principle 9: I believe with complete belief that this is the Torah, it shall not be replaced nor will the Creator blessed be His Name give us a different Torah.

This is the belief that the Torah we have today is the Torah we have for posterity, unchangeable and irreplaceable, relevant for posterity.

Principle 10: I believe with complete belief that the Creator blessed be His Name knows all the actions of every human and all their thoughts, as it is said, "He produces the hearts of them all and discerns all their doings" (Psalm 33:15).

This is the belief in Hashem's omniscience. Since His Divine Providence determines everything, no thought, utterance or occurrence in the universe is unknown to Him.

Principle 11: I believe with complete belief that the Creator blessed be His Name rewards those who observe His commandments and punishes those transgress His commandments.

This is our belief in reward and punishment as well as our belief in mankind's free will to do good or evil, for there can be no concept of reward and punishment outside the context of free will, if there is the slightest coercion in either direction.

Principle 12: I believe with complete belief in the coming of the Messiah, and even though he tarries, I will nonetheless await him every day, whenever he comes.

We believe that the Messiah has not yet come, but we eagerly anticipate his arrival together with the advent of the Messianic era that includes the *Geula*, the full redemption of our people, the ingathering of the exiles to our holy homeland of Israel and the rebuilding of our Holy Temple in Jerusalem.

Principle 13: I believe with complete belief that there will be a resurrection of the dead at the prescribed time that the

Creator wills, blessed be His Name and may He be exalted forever and ever.

We believe that death as we know it today is a passing stage and not terminal, for we believe in the resurrection of the dead.

Introductory Chapter

This chapter explains why learning the Thirteen Principles of Emuna is so vital

Ask anyone, Jewish or not, if they believe in God. Many people will answer in the affirmative. Now, ask one of the believers what it means to believe in God. Few will give you a clear answer.

Let's go a step further. Ask any Jew, regardless of religious affiliation or orientation, if he or she believes in God. A huge majority will answer yes. Now ask them what Jews believe in. Again, few will provide a clear answer.

At this point, the dubious brow challenge, "What are you talking about, Torah-observant Jews don't know what Jews believe in?" I'm afraid they don't. Sure, all Torah-observant Jews ostensibly eat kosher food and observe the Sabbath laws. Ask them why and they'll answer, "Because the Torah says so!" Yet, what happens in a generation of mega-temptations when many people - young and old - harbor doubts about the Torah's veracity or the relevance of the Jewish faith in the age of high-tech?

What's there to stop a so-called "observant" teenage girl from locking herself in her bedroom and text-messaging on Shabbat? What's there to prevent the "observant" businessman from compromising the Torah's laws of integrity in commerce? What can possibly prevent the "observant" young man from changing his clothes and driving to a destination outside the community's watchful eye and doing something that the Torah tells him is wrong? Where's the emergency protection against temper tantrums, anxiety, fear, depression and other negative emotions?

Without *emuna*, the pure and complete faith in the Almighty, one's observance of Torah is ever so vulnerable. Therefore, the evil inclination will do everything to prevent a person from strengthening emuna. Why? With emuna, a person derives conviction, commitment, inner strength and above all, inner peace. He or she becomes free and breaks loose from the choking clutches of the evil inclination, the "dark side" as Kabbalah calls it, because it's the source of all spiritual impurity, emotional darkness and negative feelings, the total opposite of "the illuminated side", which is the source of holiness and positive emotions such as happiness and inner peace.

The Almighty declared on Mount Sinai, on the occasion of granting the Torah to the Jewish People with Moses and two million other witnesses present, and said, "I am the Lord your God who took you out of the land of Egypt and the house of bondage" (Exodus 20:2). This is the first of the Ten Commandments and the *mitzva* (commandment) of emuna, the most important of the 613 commandments of the Torah.

A professor of literature or a linguist might protest and claim that the above passage is merely a statement, not a commandment. Our great sage Nachmanides (aka Ramban, 1194-1270 CE) begs to differ. In his elucidation of the abovementioned passage he says, "This utterance is a positive commandment[2]; the declaration of 'I am the Lord your God' commands us to know and believe that there

---

[2] Of the Torah's 613 commandments, 248 are "positive commandments" that call for positive action while 365 are "negative commandments" that require a person to refrain from doing a certain action. By action, we refer to thought and speech as well as deeds.

is a God – **Hashem -** and He is the One who took us out of Egypt." Since the beginning of time, He has not changed.

Beginning with the first of the Ten Commandments, and then gleaning the entire Torah, the Rambam summarized the thirteen principles of our belief in the Almighty, commonly known as "**The Thirteen Principles of Emuna**". Few people know them by heart and even fewer – including Torah observant Jews – live by them. Happiness and inner peace are two of the key rewards in living by the thirteen principles. Conversely, any breach of happiness or inner peace is a sign that one's emuna needs reinforcement.

The entire purpose of this modest book, which one can carry in a pocket or purse, is to enable the reader to attain the happiness and inner peace that is unattainable elsewhere, by offering a clear and practical guide to the thirteen principles, which any individual between the ages of 12-120 can readily comprehend and internalize.

Truth and Emuna

A person might have doubts about emuna. No one wants to waste time learning something that's not true. How do we know that emuna is true?

The Zohar teaches that the moment the soul leaves the body, it utters a cry that's heard from one end of the spiritual realm to the other, for it sees the Divine Presence and suffers tremendous remorse and embarrassment that it squandered a valuable life on earth that was meant to search for and discover truth.

A soul that connects to the Almighty in this world will discover truth. Why?

"Hashem is One and His Name is One" (Zachariah 14:9); "The Lord our God is truth" (Jeremiah 10:10). From juxtaposing these two passages, we learn that Hashem is One and Hashem is truth (Zohar III:51b). There is no truth exclusive of Hashem for He alone is truth (Daniel 4:34), His Name is truth (Psalm 31:6) and His Torah is truth (Psalm 119:142).

When Moses ascends Mount Sinai and encounters Hashem as revealed in the burning bush, he asks to know Hashem's holy Name. The Almighty responds, "I am that I am" (see Exodus 3:14), one of the seven holy Names that may not be erased (see Shulchan Aruch, Yora Deah, 266:9).

"I am" in Hebrew is *ehyeh* which has a numerical equivalent of 21 (Hebrew letters aleph-hey-yud-hey: aleph=1, hey=5, yud=10, hey=5, together=21). "I am that I am" can therefore be converted into a mathematical equation. According to tradition, "that" - *asher* in Hebrew - signifies multiplication (see Genesis 30:13), "I am that I am" may now be converted to 21x21, which equals 441. The Hebrew letter "aleph" has the value of 1, the letter "mem" has the value of 40, and the letter "taf" has the value of 400. *Emet*, aleph-mem-taf – is the Hebrew word for "truth", exactly 441.

To sum things up neatly, "I am that I am", Hashem's name is truth, just as 21x21=441.

The reason that Hashem chose "truth" as the signature of His holy Name is because any forgery is readily apparent. Anything other than 100% truth is a counterfeit, and not Hashem.

My esteemed teacher and mentor, the holy Melitzer Rebbe shlit"a, teaches two important rules about truth:

1. 99% truth is 100% a lie.

2. 100 lies are not a refutation of one truth.

Why aren't we all happy and emotionally healthy? Even more so, why aren't all religious people happy and emotionally healthy? They apparently have the advantage of Torah at their disposal, and the Torah is the manual for maintaining a healthy soul. Let's go a step further: why do people do immoral and dishonest acts? Once again, how can a so-called "religious" person be cruel, dishonest or immoral when he or she professes to be Torah-observant?

The answer to the above riddle is clear: the notion of emuna is rarely clarified in people's minds. Emuna loses all meaning as soon as it's severed – even in the slightest – from the truth. Since truth is Hashem's signature, the slightest deviation or alteration of the truth is a falsification of the Divine signature, a counterfeit.

With a lack of knowledge or total misconception of what truth is, a person cannot be happy or fulfilled. He or she won't know what they're doing on earth. They'll be lost, with no clear direction. Even if they're apparently successful in their non-truth-oriented endeavor, someone or something always comes along to give them a rude awakening. Many people pursue money for money's sake; while scoffing at that folly, an old Chassidic expression says, "Either Hashem takes the money away from the person or the person away from the money; shrouds need no pockets." Money, or any other amenity, can be a means toward accomplishing a mission but it is never one's true mission on earth.

The desire to accomplish our mission on earth and to live meaningful lives is therefore a huge incentive to learn the principles of emuna and ingrain them in our being to the extent that they become second nature, where we live them and breathe them.

The Thirteen Principles of Emuna open up new vistas for an individual, for they are the gate to emuna and emuna is the gate to truth and Divine wisdom. One cannot circumvent emuna and then expect to attain truth and Divine wisdom, for **emuna is the sole path to truth**. Our sages therefore codified in our *Shacharit* (morning) prayer, "Truth and emuna, Divine law with no exceptions." In other words, everything Hashem does is Divine truth and Divine wisdom that defy the human intellect, and there are no exceptions.

King David therefore says in Psalm 119:86 that all Hashem's commandments are emuna; the same Psalm also says that all Hashem's commandments are truth (ibid. 151). Emuna is the prerequisite for not only observing them properly, but for finding truth itself.

Emuna teaches that even when something appears to be natural or logical, it really is not, for everything in the universe is the product of Divine will and providence of the Creator. This brings us to a level of spiritual awareness that enables us to recognize truth and thereby maximize personal potential beyond our wildest imagination, enable each of us to fulfill our respective mission on earth and to attain inner peace and lasting joy. With these incentives, we now proceed to learn the Thirteen Principles of Emuna. May Hashem help us succeed!

The First Principle: No one but Him

Principle 1: I believe with complete belief that the Creator, blessed be His Name, is Creator and Director of all the creations, and He alone did, does and will do every deed.

This is the belief in the existence of the Creator and that He is the life force behind all of creation; nothing can exist without His will, from the mega-galaxies to the tiniest parts of an atom. The Creator makes everything happen and nothing can happen or exist against His will or without Him. This first principle of emuna corresponds to the first of the Ten Commandments, "I Am the Lord your God" (Exodus 20:2). As such, it is a commandment for all of humanity, not just for the Jewish People.

Our first principle is beautifully exemplified by a story about one of Jerusalem's best-known tzaddikim from this past generation, Rebbe Asher "Usher" Freund osb"m (1910-2004). Rebbe Usher was in the woods on the outskirts of Jerusalem in personal prayer. He was repeatedly shouting, "It's not Menashe! It's not Menashe!" Another person who knew Rebbe Usher heard the shouts and came running in his direction to see if anything was wrong. Rebbe Usher continued shouting, "It's not Menashe! It's not Menashe!"

"Is something wrong, Rebbe? Why are shouting like this?"

Rebbe Usher turned to the young man and said, "A person named Menashe took money away from me that I had earmarked for poor people. I don't want a single shred of animosity to penetrate my heart, especially since the very first thing we believe in is that Hashem alone did, does and will do every deed. So instead of any ill-feeling against another human being, I have to drive into my heart that it's not Menashe, it's Hashem!"

Rebbe Usher's entire life was devoted to helping poor people, so losing this money was more painful to him than losing his health. Yet, he would not let himself succumb to the slightest of negative emotions, for in his eyes, a negative emotion was tantamount to a person saying that he or she is displeased with the way the Creator runs the world, Heaven forbid. Contrastingly, the type of positivity and optimism that come from genuine emuna are a statement that a person is delighted with the way the Creator runs the world, a level that Rebbe Usher Freund would not let himself fall from, no matter what the adversity and hardships that life presented him with, and there were plenty of them.

The first of the Rambam's Thirteen Principles of Emuna teaches us that Hashem alone is Creator and Director of the entire universe and He alone did, does and will do every deed. Nothing in all of creation, whether in the physical or spiritual realm, can happen without Hashem.

The amazing practical advantage of knowing that there's nothing but Hashem and that everything comes from Hashem is that it frees us from violent mood swings. Here's how:

Without knowing that there's nothing but Hashem, a person is inclined to attribute any success in life to himself and thereby become smug and arrogant. Yet, when he fails or has a setback, he becomes broken and depressed. I've witnessed this phenomenon time and again, especially with salesmen, realtors, investment brokers and athletes. When they sell an expensive property, hit gold in the stock market or win an important game, they're sailing on a cloud. But when their sales go down, investments crashes or they lose a game that they trained hard for, they crash land. Such emotional extremes wreak havoc on a person's nervous system.

In applying the first principle of emuna to everyday life, we must maintain two separate mindsets. Each of these two mindsets are true, yet each has its own proper place, as follows:

The first is the ***before the fact*** mindset, the way we think **before** we do something. Before we set out to do something, we must do our utmost to make our very best **effort**, do our best and conduct ourselves according to the laws of Torah while striving to succeed in whatever we're doing. We proceed with the knowledge that Hashem gives us **free choice** to do good or otherwise, to be lazy or diligent, to believe or not to believe and so forth.

To clarify the ***before the fact*** mindset, we must remember a significant concept known as *hishtadlus*, or **effort**. Before taking the bar or CPA exam, a prospective lawyer or CPA must study hard; they can't expect to pass the exam by sitting on the beach. Yet, their efforts must be within the framework of Torah, for *hishtadlus* does not override the obligations of Torah. Since the amount of *hishtadlus* that would be considered a person's best effort varies dramatically from individual to individual, a person should consult his or her spiritual guide in determining how much *hishtadlus* he or she must do.

If we haven't done or best effort, then we must first work harder, train harder, study harder or do whatever is in our grasp to maximize chances of success, but not more than that! If you're sitting in a train, you won't make it go faster by pushing the seat in front of you. Just as the speed of the train is beyond our control, so is the outcome of our best efforts. Therefore:

Once we've done our best effort, we shift gears into our second type of mindset, what we might call the *after the fact* mindset. Once something is over and done, we must know that the outcome is the result of **Hashem's will**. This mindset saves us untold emotional wear and tear and saves us from extreme mood-swings. We don't become elated and arrogant when we succeed, because we know that our success comes from Hashem. Conversely, we don't fall into depression when we fail and we refrain from persecuting ourselves or blaming others, for we know that Hashem willed that we fail. Like Rebbe Usher reminded himself constantly, "He alone did, does and will do every deed."

When we ponder the first principle and the story about Rebbe Usher, we begin to realize how the first point of emuna alone works wonders for our emotional health.

Once again, don't ever confuse the two mindsets. Don't say before you do something that you're not responsible, because Hashem will make you succeed or fail as He wishes anyway. You must do your best. Yet, after the fact, don't blame and persecute yourself if you fail, just thank Hashem for the setback for it is surely a growth opportunity that a loving Father in Heaven gives to His beloved son or daughter. As a loving Father, everything He does will always be for the very best, whether or not we understand how or why.

Since Hashem alone is Creator and Director of the entire universe and He alone did, does and will do every deed, nothing in all of creation, whether in the physical or spiritual realm, can happen without Him.

Let's take a tangible macro look at Hashem's phenomenal Divine Providence, His personal direction of all creation. This gives us a glimpse of His power and glory.

The eight planets in our solar system, of which Planet Earth is one, speed around the sun in incredible speeds. In comparison, if you've ever driven a car at 120 mph, you know how fast that is. When you take off on a jet flight, you're hustling down the runway at about 170 mph. Pretty fast, eh? When compared to the planets, it's less than snail's pace. Mercury, the fast of the planets, circles the sun at a whopping 107,000 miles an hour, 630 times faster than a fast jetliner at takeoff and 139 times faster than the speed of sound.

Planet Earth, somewhat slower than Mercury, "only" speeds through space at 66,615 mph, "only" 87 times faster than the speed of sound.

Jupiter, the biggest planet, is 1,321 times bigger than planet earth. It's also 2.5 times more massive than all the rest of the planets in the Solar System combined.

Jupiter, the big heavy planet, still orbits at a speed of 8 miles/second or approximately 29,000 mph.

In weight equivalent, a collision between Jupiter and Planet Earth would be equivalent to a collision between an 18-wheeler Mac truck and a 60-pound child, not at 50 mph but at tens of thousands of miles per hour; nothing would remain of planet earth!

Look how many accidents there are on our highways every day! But the fact that our planet exists is proof that there's never been an accident in the solar system in nearly 6,000 years of creation! How can it be that no planet has ever veered from its lane?

Hashem in His magnificent wisdom and majesty gives the sun a prodigious gravitational force that holds each planet in its own elliptical orbit.

We mentioned how gigantic Jupiter is. The sun is 1,000 times bigger than Jupiter.

Planet Earth in the Solar System is like a pebble in Yankee Stadium. Our Solar System is part of the Milky Way Galaxy, but the Milky Way is 4.12 septillion times more massive than our Solar System. As we go further in space, we encounter more galaxies, among which the Milky Way is less than a grain of sand.

Even with this small discourse, we don't even scratch the surface of describing Hashem's glory. From His lofty throne of a magnitude that defies grasp of the human brain, Hashem descends all the way trillions of light years (one light year is 5.88 trillion miles!) back down through the superclusters, through the galaxies, through the Milky Way, through our Solar system, down to Planet Earth, to our continent, country, home town and right to our back yard to feed a ladybug in the garden.

Are you beginning to understand the mind-boggling magnitude of Divine Providence? We haven't scratched the surface yet.

Yes, that's Hashem Himself personally deciding what that ladybug will have for breakfast. He alone did, does and will do every deed. He alone makes sure that silkworms grow in the neighborhood of mulberry trees, for they thrive on mulberry leaves. Since Hashem takes such good care of a lady bug or a silkworm, imagine what He does for each of us, His beloved children!

Now, let's take a closer look at Hashem's Divine Providence in micro.

The Gemara teaches that each of us is an entire universe. So just as we looked at Hashem's magnificent universe in macro, extending from every individual creation on earth to the octillionth light year in space and beyond, past mega-galaxies and superclusters, let's now take a glance in reverse, in micro, starting with ourselves.

In micro, it's much easier to speak in metric terms, so please excuse me as I switch terminology. At one meter away from each other, we see each other in our entirety.

Let's get closer and imagine that our eyes have magnifying and microscopic capabilities. At 1 millimeter (1 meter = 1,000 millimeters) away from each other, we can discern the parts of the eye – the pupil, iris and retina. If we move another ten times closer to the distance of 100 micrometers, we'll see blood vessels in the eye that look like the Mississippi River and blood cells that look like ferry boats floating with the current. Even closer, at the distance of ten micrometers, each blood cell looks like a massive planet and at one micrometer, we can see chromosomes within the blood cell. Take a deep breath…

Once again, we have to change terminology and move over to nanometers, which are one-thousandth of a micrometer, or one-millionth of a millimeter, or one-trillionth of a meter.

At a tenth of a micrometer, or 100 nanometers, a chromosome looks like a transparent snake whose spine is the DNA chain. An Angstrom unit is 10 times smaller than a nanometer, a picometer is 100 times smaller than an Angstrom but a femtometer is 100,000 times smaller than an Angstrom. To view individual atoms, this is how far we must descend. We won't even mention how deep we must delve into the micro-miniscule realm to split atoms into protons, neutrons and electrons, for such in-depth contemplation is liable to make anyone dizzy.

That's no one other than Hashem deciding that there will always be eight protons in the nucleus of every atom of oxygen. Hashem alone decides which atoms will compose which molecules that become part of our DNA, which in turn becomes part of our chromosomes to determine whether we'll have blue eyes or brown, blond hair or brown, white skin or dark, tall or short, lactose-intolerant or not and a myriad of other traits.

The same Almighty Creator who creates, controls, operates and determines the fate of super-galaxies is the same Holy Father in Heaven that personally designs each snowflake and human thumbprint. We've only taken a miniscule glimpse at the mind-boggling extent of Divine Providence. He alone did, does and will do every deed. Nothing in all of creation, whether in the physical or spiritual realm, can happen without Hashem.

Instead of investing our energy in performing our life's mission on earth, many of us waste time, effort, emotional health and wellbeing thinking that we run the world. We waste our time watching and listening to the news. We waste our time writing letters to editors, commenting on news articles and chatting aimlessly on social media. Many of us really think we run the world and then wonder why we're frustrated and depressed.

My esteemed and beloved Rosh Yeshiva, Rabbi Noah Weinberg of saintly and blessed memory used to tell us, "Move aside and let Hashem run the world." He said that the best thing a person could do is to get out of Hashem's way, and to do his own job. That is the key to being happy.

Three words from the Torah embody the entire first principle of emuna – **Ein Od Milvado** (Deuteronomy 4:35), "there is nothing but Him", teaching us that there is no one or nothing that causes anything to happen in the world outside of Hashem. A creation might do something positive or negative, but it is only an agent of Divine will and providence.

In his classic book *Nefesh HaChaim*, Rebbe Chaim of Volozhyn presents us the greatest life insurance policy ever issued, and at no cost (see Section 3, Chapter 12); he says: "Here is a prodigious and wonderful ploy to nullify all stern judgments and other forces that a person cannot control, to the extent that they will have no effect on that person at all, when the individual firmly embeds in his heart that:

"Hashem is the true God and there is no one but Him – *Ein Od Milvado* – there is no power on earth or in the entire universe but Him, and everything is filled

with His simple oneness, may His Name be blessed.

"One must nullify in his heart any thought to the contrary, that there is any power of will in the world other than His, and cling to the Almighty and to Him alone, blessed is His Name; then, He will suffice to nullify all powers or desires in the world so that they will be rendered powerless against the individual."

In simple terms, as soon as a person internalizes the concept of *Ein Od Milvado* – there is no power on earth or in the entire universe but The Almighty – and believes with all his heart that no one can harm a hair on his or her head without Divine sanction, then no power in the universe can harm them in the slightest.

Ein Od Milvado are therefore the three most important words a person should know, for they are the essence of the first and most important tenet of the Rambam's Thirteen Principles of Emuna, the foundation of pure and complete belief in Hashem:

"I believe with full belief that the Creator, blessed be His Name, is Creator and Director of all the creations, and He alone did, does and will do every deed."

You can attain true inner peace by internalizing three words - ***Ein Od Milvado*** - there is no one but Him. Hashem is everything. We need not look anywhere else for anything we need in material or spiritual abundance and salvation. For anyone who yearns for inner peace, Hashem is your one-stop shopping address.

Many people are skeptical when I tell them this. You do believe that a diabetic individual sees a dramatic improvement in health by getting off of junk food and sugar, and by going on a high-fiber natural diet rich in nutrients. If he adds a few minutes of exercise every day, he'll further guarantee his good health. That's a no-brainer and a simple matter of discipline, especially when the diabetic realizes that his life depends on it.

The same principle applies to the soul. By focusing on and internalizing the three simple words which encapsulate our first principle of emuna, namely that Hashem, blessed be His Name, is Creator and Director of every creation, and He alone did, does and will do every deed, you'll rid yourself of stress, anxiety, sadness and depression. I almost forgot despair and disappointment, as well as anger and jealousy. Our first

principle of emuna therefore paves the way
to lasting inner peace.

The Second Principle: Divine Unity

Principle 2: I believe with complete belief that the Creator blessed be His Name is One and there is no unity like Him under any circumstances and He alone is our God, past, present and future.

This is the belief that the Creator is One perfect inseparable whole with no co-deities in any way, independent of everyone and everything and perfectly unified, as we say in the *Shema* prayer, "Here O Israel, the Lord our God, the Lord is One" (Deuteronomy 6:4).

Some of history's most brilliant minds have misconstrued the concept of "One prefect inseparable whole...perfectly unified." We are talking about the very core of monotheism. The principle of Divine Unity is therefore universal, not just Jewish. The reason that great minds and intellectuals so frequently fail to understand the notion of Divine Unity is because it defies intellect.

Emuna in general and the principle of Divine Unity in particular only begin where intellect leaves off.

A poignant story in the Gemara (Tractate Chagiga 14b) highlights the importance learning emuna, despite one's intellect however lofty it might be, and the vital significance of believing in Divine Unity. The story is much deeper than meets the eye, but we'll try to reveal with Hashem's help what lies beneath its layers of allegory, as follows:

"Four people entered an orchard." The Gemara is talking about the four greatest minds of the generation of Tannaic sages who lived in the difficult times of the cruel Roman Occupation in Israel, between the destruction of the Second Holy Temple and the Bar Cochba revolt. These were Rebbe Akiva, Ben Azai, Ben Zoma, and Elisha ben Abuya. The "orchard" is a metaphor of the deepest Kabbalistic wisdom and secrets that are light years beyond the upper limits of human intellect. These four wise men first purified themselves then made ascents of the soul by invoking the Ineffable Name.

Rebbe Akiva warned the others, "When you get to the place of the marble stones, don't exclaim, 'Water, water!'" In the Temple, there were marble floors that looked just like waves of water. Rebbe Akiva knew that there was no physicality in the Upper Realm, and that the illusion of a partition between the physical realm and the spiritual real was an image of the marble that went into the construction of the Holy Temple, which was so glimmering that it looked like water. Well prepared for what he was about to see, Rebbe Akiva entered the Upper Realm peacefully and exited peacefully.

His three colleagues were not so fortunate. With one small glimpse of the purely spiritual realm, where G-dliness is not concealed like it is in the physical realm, Ben Azai's soul left him to cling to the Creator and he died. Ben Zoma could not stand the intense illumination of Divine light and went insane. Elisha ben Abuya saw two seemingly opposing forces, mercy and stern judgment, so he thought that there were multiple forces Above, Heaven forbid, and became a heretic.

Don't think that we're talking about regular people. Ben Azai and Ben Zoma were two of the greatest minds that ever lived. Elisha ben Abuya was the revered teacher of Rebbe Meir Baal Haness, before the latter became a pupil of Rebbe Akiva and Rebbe Yishmael. One lost his life; one lost his mind and the third lost his faith. What was the difference between them and Rebbe Akiva?

Rebbe Akiva studied under the tutelage of the two the greatest scholars of the generation, Rebbe Yehoshua ben Chanania and Rebbe Eliezer "The Great" ben Horkonos, from whom stem the backbone the entire Talmud. Yet, he left them to spend 22 years learning with Nachum Ish Gamzu, who barely said one *halacha*, one religious law, in the entire Talmud. Why?

Nachum Ish Gamzu was a giant of emuna. He lived the Rambam's Principles nearly ten centuries before the Rambam compiled them. Nachum Ish Gamzu taught Rebbe Akiva emuna, that everything is from Hashem and that Hashem is One. Rebbe Akiva knew that without emuna, his Torah learning would be incomplete, academic, and not engraved on the fibers of his soul. He also knew that if he relied on intellect, he wouldn't be able to comprehend the Divine wisdom of Torah and its secrets.

Rebbe Akiva, better prepared in emuna than any of his contemporaries, cast intellect aside when entering the Upper Realm. He knew that he was entering a threshold that could be both dangerous and confusing, as it was to his colleagues. All he did was focus on the Oneness of Hashem; Hashem is One. The truth of Hashem's Unity was worth sacrificing his life for, which he did, as we'll soon see.

Where people deny the Oneness of the Creator or His existence at all, Heaven forbid, the world is a very dark place as we see in everything going on around us.

The Sfas Emes writes (Parshas Miketz, 5634), that when the light of Torah is revealed in the world, darkness is dispersed and the Oneness of Hashem – Divine unity – becomes apparent.

Divine unity emanates a splendid illumination in the world. This is not a physical light that is measured in so many watts, angstroms or nanometers, but spiritual light. Spiritual lights are blessings, the bestowing of abundance in the world of all types. According to Kabbalah, any deficiency in the world is the result of an absence of Divine light. In that vein, King

David says, "There is no deficiency for those who awe Him" (Psalm 34:10). The holy language of Biblical Hebrew is not only a deep goldmine of secrets but economical in words as well. King David says, "For those who awe Him" – five words; in Biblical Hebrew, it's only one word, *li'rayav*. By scrambling the letters, we derive the two words, *li or*, which means "I have light." King David is hereby hinting that one who awes Hashem merits Divine illumination and therefore lacks nothing.

Just as our first principle of emuna corresponds to the first of the Ten Commandments, "I Am the Lord your God" (Exodus 20:2), our second principle corresponds to the second of the Ten Commandments, "You shall have no other gods but Me" (ibid.). We must emphasize that this too is a commandment for all of humanity, not just for the Jewish People.

The concept of Divine unity is what constitutes the purest form of monotheism, for it is mutually exclusive with any type of idolatry or paganism. What's more, the concept of Divine unity rules out any type of "partnership", *shituf*, where a person believes in God but he or she also believes in some additional entity with supposed godly powers.

Where do the idolaters make their mistake? "Idolatry" sounds like a stiff term and the vast majority of people in the world would be fiercely insulted if someone referred to them as an idolater. Yet, the moment anyone attributes any power to anyone or anything other than the Creator, he or she is compromising Divine unity. Here's an example:

After the U.S. presidential election in November of 2020, a lividly upset person approached me. Before I had a chance to say hello or ask what's wrong, he began ranting, "Rabbi, the President lost the election! What's going to be with Israel? We're in big trouble! How can the American government let the election be stolen like that? It's terrible…"

I looked at the man's hat and beard. He wore a long black coat as well. "Do you believe in Hashem?" I asked.

"Of course, I do!" the man bellowed back. "Can't you see?" he said to me, referring to his appearance.

"Then do you think that the Almighty is some frail great-grandma in the sky who is too weak to intervene in the American presidential elections, Heaven forbid?"

The man, well-educated in Torah, countered capably, "What about free choice? Hashem doesn't take away our free choice." He had a good point, but not good enough, for it was deficient in emuna.

"You're correct," I answered, "partially. Fifty percent correct is one-hundred percent wrong. We have two mindsets: before we do something, we try our best to do what's right and to do our best. But once it's done, the outcome is Hashem's will. If Hashem willed that the challenger shall defeat the incumbent, then it doesn't matter what people do or how they vote, the incumbent will not win."

The above narrative is a small but common example how most people, despite their religiosity and Torah education, never fully learned and internalized the concept of Hashem's unity.

The gentleman who approached me on the street believes with all his heart that the Creator is good and does only good. He therefore suffers a spiritual setback, and subsequently an emotional setback that manifests itself in anxiety, depression, disappointment and/or anger when he encounters unfavorable situations or phenomena, such as a pandemic or his candidate losing an election.

Would you call such a person an idolater? He eats kosher food, observes the Sabbath and sends his children to the best Torah schools.

The classic 15th Century CE book of faith, *Sefer Ha'Ikarim* by Rabbi Yoseph Albo, states that any attributing of power to anything or anyone other than Hashem is tantamount to believing in other gods – idolatry (see Third Discourse, Ch. 18). *Sefer Ha'Ikarim* also refutes the philosophical notion that the Creator created the world but no longer intervenes in its daily functioning, Heaven forbid. Such an attitude is a denial of Divine Providence as well as Divine unity.

Continuing this line of thought, the *Sefer Ha'Ikarim* refers to the manner whereby a person makes a living and says that if a person thinks that he or she can find abundance outside the framework of Divine will, they are in fact erecting an idol!

Rebbe Nachman of Breslev mirrors the same concept when he writes that the pursuit of income outside the framework of emuna is in itself self-defeating, for it will cause deficiency, for in effect, this too is idolatry (see Likutei Moharan I: 40). Rebbe Nachman refers to the attempts to amass money outside the limitations of Torah as false gods, when the lust for money overrides Divine law, Heaven forbid.

Throughout our history, our ancestors preferred to sacrifice their lives rather than deny the principle of Divine unity. They were even offered fabulous rewards of fame and fortune if they'd simply compromise Divine unity and accept a religion that believes in the Almighty but adds an additional co-deity or two. No compromise, ever!

One of our most moving High Holiday prayers, *Unetana Tokef*, was the result of Rabbi Amnon of Mainz (13th Century CE Germany) and his refusal to compromise his faith. Rabbi Amnon, a nobleman and advisor to the Duke of Mainz, refused the Duke's insistence that he convert. Rather than accede to the Duke's demands, Rabbi Amnon had his fingers and toes chopped off, one by one. After each time another finger or toe was chopped off, the Duke asked Rabbi Amnon if he still persists in his stubborn belief; he did. It was the day before Rosh Hashanah.

The next day, Rabbi Amnon asked to be taken to synagogue. He was placed on a stretcher, with his fingers and toes wrapped in cloth by his side. He asked permission to be placed in front of the Holy Ark so he could sanctify the Divine Name. When he said, "He is our God, there is no other," his last ounce of strength left him and he returned his soul to its Maker.

Martyrs, from the Roman gallows to the Holocaust gas chambers went to their deaths declaring in their final breath, "Hear O Israel, the Lord our God, the Lord is One" (Deuteronomy 6:4). This holy passage teaches us the oneness of Hashem.

The Romans imprisoned and tried Rebbe Akiva for teaching Torah in public, a "criminal" act according to their evil decrees. In the early evening hours, they tortured him to death, ripping off his skin with iron rakes in an unprecedentedly excruciating form of torture that no less than a Satan could improvise. Quickly losing his life force, Rebbe Akiva began to say the

Shema, "Hear O Israel, the Lord our God, the Lord is One"; as he called out One in a prolonged fashion, his martyred soul departed from this world.

Like the gentleman who approached me on the street who was upset about the election results, people find difficulty in attributing everything to the Almighty. Since the first principle of emuna is not firmly engrained in their psyche, namely that everything comes from Hashem past, present and future, it's virtually impossible for them to believe in Divine unity. Subconsciously or even consciously, they ask themselves, "How can a loving Father in Heaven be abusive (Heaven forbid) to His children? Why does He enable evil in the world? How can the same Creator be One?"

Hashem answers that question Himself: "I form the light, and create darkness; I make peace, and create evil; I am Hashem, that does all these things" (Isaiah 45:7). Hashem's oneness is inherent in all of creation from the very first day when He created the opposing powers of light and darkness.

In order to understand the concept of Divine unity with the limits of our sorely constricted human intellects, we must realize that emuna begins where intellect ends. Sometimes, we understand that pain and suffering are a gift from Above for our ultimate benefit.

A soldier in an elite combat unit understands that his training will be arduous and his commanders tough and seemingly insensitive. He also knows that his commander's worst nightmare is to bring him home from the war in a body bag. That soldier is willing to suffer in order to win the war and come home alive.

Look who's standing behind a champion athlete and you'll find a very harsh coach who at times looks outright sadistic. Why does the coach make his or her athlete suffer so much with no-compromise, tax-the-limits training? One doesn't win games and earn gold medals eating chocolate ice-cream.

With the above in mind, when we don't understand why we experience tribulations and hardships, we must believe that they are all for our ultimate benefit, to strengthen our emuna and to purify our souls. Therefore, our second principle of emuna, Divine unity, goes hand in hand with the belief that everything Hashem does is for the very best.

When combining our first two principles of emuna, that everything is from Hashem and that everything is for the best, our positivity surges and our negative emotions disappear. As such, the more we internalize our first two principles of emuna, the closer we get to realizing our dream of inner peace and lasting happiness.

The Third Principle: Incorporeal

Principle 3: I believe with complete belief that the Creator blessed be His Name is not a body, nor can any physical entity comprehend Him. He is incorporeal, with no image whatsoever.

The Creator defies any description, nor can a mortal understand Him or His workings in any way. Kabbalistic terminology refers to Hashem as ***Ein Sof***, "The Infinite", for there is nothing tangible or finite about Hashem. Since the human intellect is both tangible and finite, it can neither grasp Hashem nor comprehend His incorporeality. Yet, since emuna transcends intellect and begins where intellect ends, emuna is the prerequisite for getting to know Hashem in any way, in accordance with each soul's individual potential and efforts in acquiring spiritual awareness.

This third principle of emuna, where we learn that no physical entity can comprehend Hashem, is regarded by many of our sages as the most difficult to learn, if not the most difficult of all the thirteen for a person to accept, because of four main hurdles:

First, as long as a person prioritizes bodily needs and appetites over the soul's needs, he or she won't be able to accept any commandment or limitation to bodily desires.

Second, a person's ego stands in the way of accepting any concept that goes beyond ego's ability to understand, for it is an admission that the person cannot control everything in life, and this is difficult for a human to admit.

Third, since the beginning of time, the nations of the world have challenged Jews and anyone else who accepts this principle, doing everything in their power, including subjugation, torture and outright attempts at annihilation to prevent the belief in the noncorporeal God and Creator.

Fourth, since the Torah itself refers to the Almighty in tangible imagery, people make the mistake of thinking that there is some tangible, albeit sublime, nature to the Creator, Heaven forbid.

Let's do examine each of these four hurdles and show how we can capably jump over them in our quest to learn and internalize our third principle of emuna.

Hurdle #1: Bodily Appetites

As we explained in our introductory chapter, an animal lacks both a human soul and a Divine soul. My esteemed and beloved teacher the Melitzer Rebbe shlit'a quips, "A cow doesn't understand how a clock works; the Creator created her in this limited fashion. By the same token, He created us in a limited fashion, that we cannot comprehend Him, otherwise we wouldn't need emuna."

All a cow cares is that she's hungry and it's feeding time, or that she needs someone to milk her and it's milking time. She doesn't need to wear a Seiko or a Casio around her neck nor know how the watch works.

The Creator, Whose essence defies any and all comprehension, created us in a limited manner as well, although less limited than a cow, a dog or a horse. Even though animals can be trained, their training is instinctual, developing the animal's instinct to its highest potential, for this is the upper limits of an animal soul. Yet, no animal can learn to reason, for reason falls within the realm of the human soul.

To activate the Divine soul and begin learning emuna in general and the third principle in particular, one must override the animal soul. Once again, as we learned in the introductory chapter, the animal soul is a prodigious gravitational force that pulls the human soul down. Said simply, as long as the body is in the way, the soul doesn't stand much of a chance in getting its way.

Let's elaborate. A person loves cheeseburgers. If the body gets its way, the person won't want to hear anything about the Torah's prohibition of eating, enjoying or cooking milk and meat together. Yet, if the soul's love for Hashem overrides the body's love for cheeseburgers, it can override the body, accept Torah and learn emuna. The same thing goes for any other type of bodily appetite.

So how do most people react? They don't want the Creator or the Torah telling them what to do. They therefore do one of two things: either they deny the truth of the Creator and His Torah altogether and remove the spiritual regulatory entity that tells the how to live their lives; or, they invent a new belief system, such as "conservatism" or "reformism" that eases their conscience and accommodates all their bodily appetites. This is a classic example of shooting the arrow, then drawing a bullseye around wherever it lands. Needless to say, that's not truth. Then, people can't understand why they harbor so much inner turmoil and negative emotions, again easing their conscience by blaming others.

Consequently, in order to straddle the first hurdle of our bodily appetites getting in the way of learning our third principle of emuna, we must tweak our body-soul priorities and not allow physical amenities – as strong as they are – to get in the way of truth. Happy is the individual who jumps over this hurdle.

Hurdle #2: Ego

For a person to accept the third principle of emuna, namely, that the Creator is not a body, nor can any human comprehend Him for He is incorporeal, with no image whatsoever, physical or otherwise, he or she must cast ego aside. Most people cannot do this. Even many religious people with apparent emuna are still far away from accepting the principle that they cannot comprehend Hashem. How?

The Koznitzer Maggid explains (Avodas Yisroel, Parshas Vayakhel-

Pekudei) that a person's fear of punishment or desire for reward in this world is really physically-oriented, not spiritually oriented, when the person's goal is to enhance pleasure and avoid displeasure in this world. Therefore, if pleasure-seeking and pain avoidance is the extent of a person's so-called "emuna", it won't be strong enough to weather challenges and tribulations.

Although fear of punishment is entry-level Torah observance, it's still bound in ego, when a person understands that it's better to forego a temptation rather than suffer its consequences. Even though he or she is laudably observing the Torah, their motivation is nonetheless ego-based. People on this level will suffer as soon as life removes them from their comfort zone.

Rebbe Schneur Zalman of Liadi goes a step further is describing the difficulty in understanding the third principle of emuna (see Tanya, Igeret Hakodesh, Ch.3). He explains that one must first nullify one's desires for worldly amenities before one is able to grasp the concept of Divine light. The reason Divine wisdom is not perceivable to the human intellect is because it is loftier than anything we can imagine, even spiritually, for the ***Ein Sof***, the core of

Godliness is naught, transcending all spiritual realms and doing everything for the good.

The scientific world especially has difficulty in overcoming the ego hurdle, for all their theories of creation, including the "Big-Bang" theory, are based on the presumption of primordial matter existing before the world was created. Yet, hand in hand with our third principle of emuna is the belief that the world was created *yesh-me'ayin*, Hebrew for ex nihilo. As the Baal Hatanya states (ibid.), everything stems from His blessed wisdom, which is the source of all life and creation.

We complain about "control freaks", yet we are all control freaks until we admit to ourselves that there is a Creator Whom we cannot fathom and Whose Divine will is beyond our comprehension. Therefore, as soon as we put ego aside and are prepared to accept life with emuna, we overcome this second hurdle and make a major stride toward spiritual growth and inner peace.

Hurdle #3: The Nations of the World

Since the beginning of time, the nations of the world and their leaders have challenged, pursued and persecuted Jews and anyone else who accepts the principle of belief in a non-comprehensible, non-corporeal Creator. Why? Such a belief undermines their own lust for power and quest to subjugate the masses for their own benefit. Our faith has therefore come with the price tag of subjugation, torture and outright attempts at annihilation.

Nimrod, tyrannical leader of ancient Babylon, needed to establish himself as a deity to solidify his regime. Abraham, the first believer and monotheist, was a bone in Nimrod's throat. He threw Abraham into a fiery furnace. Abraham emerged unscathed.

Moses told Pharaoh in the Name of God, "Let My people Go!" Pharaoh, who like Nimrod before him tried to establish himself as a deity along with the many other deities in pagan ancient Egypt, had to deny the credibility of a non-corporeal, non-comprehensible Almighty. Pharaoh therefore responded, "Who is Hashem that I should listen to Him? I don't know Him and I will therefore not let Israel go!" (Exodus 5:2).

Let's be exacting in Pharaoh's answer. He claims that he won't listen to Hashem because he doesn't ***know*** him. Pharaoh couldn't stand the fact that there was anything in the world that he didn't know, and therefore could not accept a true God that defies human understanding.

King Solomon said that nothing is new under the sun (Ecclesiastes 1:9). How many people today have the same attitude as Pharaoh? They too won't listen to Hashem, no matter that Hashem is absolute truth, because they don't understand Him!

The whole story of Chanukah and the war against the Greeks and Hellenism centers around our third principle of emuna. The holy Rebbe Yerachmiel Yisroel Yitzchok Dancyger, aka "Yismach Yisroel" of Alexander, writes (Discourse on Chanukah) that the aim of the Greeks was to force their belief system on the People of Israel, particularly that one must not believe in anything that transcends human intellect or that mortal man cannot grasp. They utterly denied the notion of an incomprehensible, non-corporeal Creator.

The Maccabees and a few other loyal Jews vocally and vehemently warned the Jewish populace against subscribing to the false ideology and paganism of the Greeks. Nonetheless, some 95% of the Jews acquiesced to "Hellenism" – the Greek or "Hellenistic" ideas, and utterly assimilated. The Greeks took control of the Holy Temple and defiled it. They sent out a proclamation all across the Land of Israel, which declared, "Write on the horns of your cattle that you have no part in the God of Israel" (Breishis Raba, 2:5). They made every effort to erase our third principle of emuna from the Jewish psyche. By doing so, they would erase Judaism, their ultimate goal.

The miracle of the Maccabean revolt, with the few against the many and the weak against the strong, together with the purification of the Holy Temple and the miraculous discovery of the pure vial of olive oil with the High Priest's seal on it and the subsequent reconsecration ("Chanukah" in Hebrew) of the Holy Temple bear witness to the Divine intervention that defied all logic to keep the light of emuna burning to this day.

The same cycle of Egyptians and Greeks continues throughout history via Romans, Crusaders, Inquisitionists, Cossacks and Nazis all with the same design, as we say every Passover in the Haggadah, "In every generation, they rise up against us to destroy us." From the dark-side resistance to our third principle of emuna, we can imagine how prodigious the rewards are for jumping over the hurdle of the nations, modern society, political correctness and social pressure and clinging to it.

Hurdle #4: The Torah's Use of Tangible Imagery

The Torah warns (Deuteronomy 4:15), "You must carefully guard your souls, for you have not seen any image [of God]". "You must carefully guard your souls" is the passage that is cited as the command for protecting health of body and soul (see Agra D'Calla, Parshas Devorim). This warning is juxtaposed with, "… you have not seen any image" to show us that attributing any physicality or physical traits to the Almighty is dangerous to body and soul.

If so, why does the Torah itself use bodily imagery? The Torah says, "Your right hand, Hashem" (Exodus 15:6); "The eyes of Hashem" (Deuteronomy 11:12). The prophets go further and attribute bodily characteristics to Hashem, like sitting, standing and traveling, such as, "The heaven is My throne, and the earth is My footstool; where is the house that you may build for Me? And where is the place that may be My resting-place?" (Isaiah 66:1). And, "For all these things has My hand made" (ibid., 2). This is just a small sample. How do we explain this apparent contradiction to our third principle?

Our sages explain that there is no contradiction at all. Since we are finite, our brains are finite and our language is finite, the Torah must speak to us in finite imagery. "The Torah speaks in the language of humans" (Tractate Berachot 31b). The same prophet Isaiah who had no other alternative for describing his prophecies other than human language also prophesizes in the Name of Hashem, "To whom then will you liken Me, that I should be equal? said the Holy One" (Isaiah 40:25). Isaiah concludes (ibid., 28), "The everlasting God, Hashem, the Creator of every corner of the universe, never weakens or tires. His wisdom defies investigation."

Once we internalize the fact that Hashem is beyond our understanding and defies any bodily or physical characteristics, we not only jump over this fourth hurdle, but make a giant leap forward in strengthening our emuna, the emuna that our ancestors lived by and fought for the last 38 centuries since our forefather Abraham.

.

The Fourth Principle: First and Last

Principle 4: I believe with complete belief that the Creator blessed be His Name is first and last.

This is the belief that the Creator defies time and space. He is infinite and eternal, preceding the beginning of time, existing forever even after the end of time.

"Thus said Hashem, King of Israel and his Redeemer, the Lord of Hosts: I am the first, and I am the last, and beside Me there is no God" (Isaiah 44:6). Like our Third Principle of Emuna, this too is a principle beyond the grasp of human intellect. There has always been Hashem and there always will be Hashem; He Alone precedes creation and He alone prevails once creation is terminated.

The Gemara warns us not even to try and contemplate the nature of the Almighty's existence before and after creation, and says, "Do not investigate that which defies your ability to comprehend" (Chagiga 13a). The Gemara is not imploring a person to cease learning, but not to bother investigating things that no one has the answer for, such as what went on before creation and what will be once creation no longer exists, for this is hidden from the human intellect.

We must therefore ask ourselves: if investigating what preceded creation and what will follow creation is something dangerous that our sages warned against, then what is the practical purpose of the Fourth Principle and how does it bring us closer to Hashem?

King David says, "Hashem…You endure throughout all the generations; You laid the foundation of earth and the Heavens are the work of Your hands; they shall perish but You shall endure…Your years have no end" (Psalm 102:25-28).

Peace of Mind

The knowledge that Hashem is both infinite and eternal gives us peace of mind and tranquility of heart and soul in two distinct ways, as we'll soon see.

Let's compare serving Hashem to working for a flesh-and-blood employer.

Even if you love your employer, there's always a chance that he or she will sell the company to someone whom you'll have difficulty getting along with. Any number of things can happen to your boss. He can retire, change jobs or leave the company. You never know what to expect from a new boss and this certainly takes a toll on one's peace of mind.

Therefore, the first distinct way that Hashem's infinitude and eternality give us enhanced inner peace and freedom from much extraneous worry is that there's never a need to worry about regime change. Hashem is forever King; there won't be any replacement ever. What's more, even if we do get a new president, a new employer, a new boss or a new anyone who influences our life, we know that they are all nothing more than puppets whose strings the King Himself is pulling, or players on the King's chessboard who in some way are catalysts to bring us closer to Hashem.

Let's return to our example of a flesh-and-blood employer. Who knows what problems our employer has and what challenges he or she is currently dealing with? Who knows what type of personal issues they're confronting? Look at the myriad of day-to-day changing variables that influence a person's mood. One's employer or superior has just as many mood changes as anyone else. In that respect, a person always harbors a measure of underlying tension or anxiety about how the day at work will be. Will the boss smile? Will he yell? What will be?

"I am Hashem; I have not changed" (Malachi 3:6).

We can now see the second distinct way that Hashem's infinitude and eternality give us enhanced inner peace. We never need to worry about a mood change. Hashem is always the same and His expectations of us are crystal clear and constant; they too never change.

Free Choice and Consequences

People ask, "But what about the good days and the bad days? What about the wonderful times of life and the awful times of life? We learned in the first principle that everything is from Hashem, so how can we say that Hashem never changes?"

The Ariza'l addresses this same question in his magnum opus of Kabbalah, the *Eitz Chaim*. Elaborating his answer, the Ben Ish

Chai explains in *Daas U'tvuna* that Hashem surely does not change, but the good or bad that humans do trigger a cause-and-effect chain of reactions that channel Divine energy (which is all good at its source) into the direction of compassion to the right or stern judgment to the left. Let's further clarify this important concept in as simple a manner as possible.

Would you say that fire is bad or good? Imagine that you're camping out with friends on a chilly winter evening. You light a charcoal fire and then slow-roast a *finjan* (small pot) of aromatic Turkish coffee, Bedouin style. Then, as you sip the warming, welcome cup of coffee, you broil your favorite steaks over that charcoal fire. The fire seems to be your best friend...

Then, Heaven forbid, in a moment of carelessness, the tassels of your long scarf brush across the burning embers and catch fire. Your scarf burns, your new winter parka catches fire and you're suddenly in danger, Heaven forbid. The fire now seems to be your worst enemy...

The fire has not changed. The same fire that broiled the steaks is the fire that burned the scarf.

"For Hashem your God is an all-consuming fire" (Deuteronomy 4:24). As we learned in the Third Principle, Hashem defies corporeality and description, but the Torah does speak in metaphors so that we can grasp whatever knowledge of Hashem we can on our level. Hashem as a "fire" accepts a gratifying sacrifice on the altar as a fire from the Heavens descends miraculously and consumes it, as was seen daily in the Holy Temple. This is the same fire that burned the souls of Nadav and Avihu when they entered the Holy of Holies and made an unauthorized incense offering (Leviticus 10:2).

Hashem never changes. As we will learn in Principle Nine, G-d willing, His Torah never changes. Hashem tells us explicitly, "I call heaven and earth as witnesses this day, that I give you options of life and death, blessing and curse; therefore, choose life" (ibid. 30:19). Hashem gives us free will and He also informs us of the consequences.

King Solomon says that a fool's folly shall skew his way but then he blames Hashem (Proverbs 19:3). A fool smokes two packs of cigarettes a day and then is angry at Hashem because he has severe lung disease.

On the other hand, a couch potato weakling who watches movies all day long while drinking cola and eating potato chips is jealous of the weightlifter's muscles. If the couch potato would invest the effort in proper diet and exercise that the weightlifter does, he too would be strong and muscular.

Up until now, we spoke about the benefits of believing in Hashem's overall infinitude and eternality. When learning this Fourth Principle of emuna, we can also glean a wonderful specific benefit in knowing specifically that Hashem is first and an additional huge benefit in knowing that Hashem is last, as we are about to show.

Live a Longer Life

Scientific research repeatedly points to anxiety as a culprit in shortening life span. Although we haven't seen clinical research about how serenity, the opposite of anxiety, lengthens life span, we can certainly deduce that if we remove the life-shortening factor from our lives, then we'll naturally live longer lives.

Empirically, if we look at the giants of Torah and emuna in this past generation, we see an amazing pattern. Rabbi Aharon Yehuda Leib Steinman (1914-2017) lived to

103. Rabbi Shmuel Halevi Vosner (1913-2015) lived to 102. Rabbi Yosef Shalom Elyashiv (1910-2012) also lived to 102. The renowned Kabbalist Rabbi Yitzchak Kaduri (1898-2006) lived to 108, while the "Zutshka Rebbe", Rabbi Yitzchak Isaac Rosenbaum (1896-2000) lived to 104, all of saintly and blessed memory.

Each of the abovementioned *tzaddikim* (pious and righteous men) was a colossal Torah scholar of unshakable emuna. Each was a walking encyclopedia in his respective area of Torah expertise and each was a living book of ethics. How did they all live past the age of 100?

I'll answer with a parable.

A guest came to the synagogue for Shabbat. He sat down next to an elderly gentleman with a long white beard, obviously the oldest person in the congregation. During the Torah reading, the guest commented about every single person who was called to the Torah. He turned to the old man and asked, "Why is the *gabbai* (beadle) calling up the young Cohen and not the older Cohen? Why is he calling up the person who is not wearing a suit jacket? Why is he adding an extra aliya?" Every time he rattled off another question, the elderly man signaled that one shouldn't be talking during the Torah reading...

The moment the services were over, the guest raced up to the *gabbai* and in rapid succession, fired away with his questions. The gabbai answered patiently, "Young man, this is the first time I've ever seen you in our synagogue. I have been gabbai here for the last thirty-two years. To explain to you all the considerations behind who gets called up to the Torah on a particular Sabbath would require hours and even then, you wouldn't understand."

Unsatisfied with the gabbai's answer, the guest turned around to leave the synagogue. As he was leaving, the elderly congregant was retrieving his hat and walking cane from the cloakroom. The inquisitive guest said, "I hope you don't mind me asking, sir, but how old are you?"

The elderly man answered, "Ninety-five, thanks to the Almighty."

"And you still walk to synagogue? That's amazing! To what do you attribute your long life?"

"I don't ask questions about how the Almighty runs His world."

That's our parable. The five holy centenarians of this past generation didn't waste energy and emotional wear and tear on worrying how Hashem runs the world despite the fact that none of them lived easy lives, enduring war, poverty and deprivation.

Many of us are like the first-time guest in the synagogue. How old are we and how old is the universe? The universe has been here much longer than we are and the Creator has been here much longer than the universe. Yet, we have all types of questions, comments and criticisms as to how He runs his world, despite the fact, as we learned in Principle Three, that we can neither fathom Him or what He does.

With the above in mind, knowing that Hashem is first, Creator of everything Who precedes all creation, is conducive for a long life. When the Fourth Principle of Emuna is deeply embedded in a person's heart, he or she can expect to dance at the weddings of their great grandchildren, with Hashem's loving grace.

Live an Eternal Life

If knowing that Hashem is first is conducive for a long life, then knowing that Hashem is last is conducive for an eternal life.

The Gemara tells us that eventually, the world as we know it will cease to exist. Yet, as Hashem is here forever, He will still be around when nothing else is. Therefore, as Rabbi Avraham Saba explains in *Tzror Hamor*, when a person clings to the Divine Presence, even if he or she dies an early death and especially if they die a martyr's death, they merit eternal life, as the Torah says for posterity, "And those of you who are clinging to Hashem are still alive today" (Deuteronomy 4:4).

That's the great news: when a person knows that Hashem is last and clings to Him, that person's soul is here forever, may we all so merit, amen!

The Fifth Principle: To Him Only

Principle 5: I believe with complete belief that the Creator blessed be His Name is the only entity to whom it is befitting to pray, and it is not befitting to pray to anyone or anything else.

This is the foundation of monotheism, forbidding idolatry and false gods, thereby precluding worship or submission to anyone or anything else other than the Creator.

In his commentary on the Mishna in the tenth chapter of Tractate Sanhedrin, the Rambam makes it clear that Hashem is the only One who is worthy of our worship and our prayers. We should not direct any prayer or appeal to any other entity, for they are all His creations and subservient to Him, whether the angels, the stars, the planets, the elements or any of their compounds. The creations have no control or choice, and only perform Hashem's will.

A person might ask himself: "Who in this generation doesn't know that we don't bow down to idols? Who is gullible enough to believe that a statue has supernatural powers of its own?

One would be surprised how prone people are to falling in all types of traps that seem to be permissible. Remember though, that worshiping anyone or anything other than Hashem, including one of His highest-ranking archangels, already qualifies as false worship. **We pray to Him only**.

In elaborating on the Fifth Principle, we won't involve ourselves in obvious paganism and idolatry, for that is not within the scope of this book's task. Rather, we'll address the following areas where people inadvertently misdirect their prayers:

1. Celestial bodies – stars and planets;

2. Angels and heavenly servants;

3. The souls of the deceased.

Finally, in concluding our discussion of the Fifth Principle, we'll learn parameters of the Torah's command to serve Hashem innocently and whole-heartedly (see Deuteronomy 18:13), for this is the key to proper adherence to our Fifth Principle, which teaches us not only to pray to Him only, but to seek salvation from Him only.

Since the dawn of history, people have made the mistake of directing prayers and appeals to the apparent wielding forces of power in nature rather than to the One source of all power, Hashem, blessed be His Name.

The Celestial Bodies – Stars and Planets

The "Ramchal", Rabbi Moshe Chaim Luzatto (Derech Hashem, Section 2, Ch.7), teaches that the stars do influence humanity and events on earth. He notes two reasons for the existence of stars and planets: first, they act as conduits which the Creator uses to transmit spiritual forces to physical entities; and second, they act as catalyzers which the Creator uses to trigger events on earth.

According to the Ramchal, specific stars and positions of stars influence earthly phenomenon and apparently control them. This is all according to nature, cites the Ramchal. Yet, as our sages teach in the Gemara (Tractate Shabbos 156a) that Emuna is above the stars and overrides them. Rashi says specifically that prayer to Hashem uplifts a person beyond the influence of the stars.

Abraham our forefather, the first Hebrew, and the founder of monotheism, was an amazing astrologer and clairvoyant.

He could read the stars like we read the front-page headlines of a newspaper. He saw in the stars that he and his wife were not only destined to be childless, but that they even lacked the necessary physical apparatus for procreation. According to the Midrash, Hashem scolded Abraham, and told him to put aside the astrology and star-readings, and cling to simple faith. Abraham did just that, and became the forefather of many millions and the patriarch of the Jewish People.

The entire existence of the Jewish People is by virtue of Abraham's uplifting himself above the stars and natural forces while clinging to Hashem in prayer and in emuna, which defy nature. Prayer and emuna are so closely entwined that they are almost synonymous. One who prays does so because he or she believes; and, one who believes certainly prays.

Don't think for a moment that the capability of superseding nature applies to Jews only. A non-Jew who clings to emuna can thrive despite the fact that the stars might indicate otherwise. What's more, if a non-Jew fulfills the Seven Noahide Mitzvoth, he or she can attain the spiritual level of the

High Priest in the Holy Temple (see Tractate Avoda Zara 3a and Meiri's elaboration).

The Seven Noahide Mitzvoth are listed in Tractate Sanhedrin 56a; they are:

One, to believe in G-d;

Two, to refrain from any semblance of idol worship;

Three, not to engage in illicit sex;

Four, not to kill;

Five, not to steal;

Six, not to blaspheme The Almighty, heaven forbid;

Seven, to establish courts of justice.

Just as emuna is the foundation of all of Torah, it is the foundation of the Seven Noahide Mitzvoth. Noahides earn the right to bring sacrificial animal offerings to the Holy Temple (see Rambam, Laws of Kings, Ch.10:9-10) Just as their sacrificial offerings are accepted, their prayers are readily accepted and they too are capable of rising high above nature and the stars.

Angels and Heavenly Servants

The angels and heavenly servants are awe-inspiring insofar as they are spiritual entities on a loftier level that we mortals are. But, as we explained in the introductory chapter (see "Anatomy of Free Choice"), when a human overcomes formidable resistance to enable his or her Divine soul to prevail over their animal soul, they attain a higher spiritual level than the angels. We therefore need not seek any favors from the angels.

Praying to an angel, even to the highest archangel, is certainly forbidden. Although some people make direct requests of angels asking them to carry our prayers to the Heavenly Throne, our leading sages discourage such practice.

The *Sefer HaHasidim* ("Book of the Pious"), the 12th Century CE classic by Rabbi Yehuda The Pious, addresses the subject of appealing to the angels together with other types of spiritual pitfalls such as fortune-tellers and clairvoyance that even upright Jews have fallen into, but nonetheless are forbidden by Torah. He writes (*Sefer HaHasidim, 205*): "A person who appeals to angels, or spirits or sorcery of any kind will not see a favorable result, and can expect afflictions on himself or on his offspring for the rest of his life. Nor should he seek to know the future in any way. He must pray exclusively to Hashem; if he goes on a journey, he should not ask the angels make them swear to guard over him. Yet, when he puts all of his trust in Hashem, and prays only to Him, he will find that Hashem is merciful and compassionate."

Let's be exacting in the holy words of the *Sefer HaHasidim*: **when a person puts all of his trust in Hashem, and prays only to Him, he will find that Hashem is merciful and compassionate.**

The holy Shla (Asara Hilulim, Shaar Hayichud, 1) echoes the above thoughts and emphasizes that when a person prays exclusively to Hashem and doesn't appeal to or seek favors from anyone, then measure-for-measure, Hashem will personally intercede on that person's behalf. There is no better incentive to strengthen ourselves in the Fifth Principle of Emuna.

The Souls of the Deceased

The Zohar, Midrash and Gemara all cite the holy initiatives of praying at the gravesites of the righteous and of one's parents and ancestors.

Joshua had the blessing of Moses but Caleb did not. Caleb feared that he might fall under the negative influence of the ten spies who spoke slander about the Land of Israel, so he risked his life to traverse dangerous territory alone in order to pray from the holy gravesites of our patriarchs and matriarchs in the Machpelah cave, not praying to them, but asking them to intercede on his behalf (Zohar Shlach Lecha, Sota 34b).

Rashi writes (Exodus 37:36) that our matriarch Rachel was buried on the highway at Bethlehem so that her descendants in exile after the destruction of the First Temple could pray at her grave and she could pray for them. The "Meam Loez" cites a moving Midrash that describes how Joseph, now sold into slavery, tears himself away from his captors and weeps hot tears over his mother's grave.

One of our classic halachic commentators, the "Bach" (Rabbi Joel Sirkes 1561-1640) strongly approved of the practice of praying at one's ancestors' graves in times of difficulty, since their merit can intervene to help avert an unpleasant decree. Indeed, it is a common Jewish custom to visit the graves of close relatives on the anniversary of their passing (*yahrtzeit*) and to pray there.

The "Rama" (Rabbi Moses Isserles, 1530-1572) mentions the custom of praying by the gravesites of the deceased on the eve of Rosh Hashanah (Rama, Shulchan Aruch, Orach Chaim 581:4). The Chafetz Chaim adds (ibid., Mishna Brura, 27) that prayers are readily accepted by the gravesites of the holy tzaddikim but warns that one must not direct our prayers toward the dead who rest there, but rather implore Hashem to have mercy on us for their sake. In this respect, anything in the nature of conjuring up souls of the deceased by way of seances and the like is utterly forbidden.

There was a time in the IDF when seances became extremely popular. During the First Lebanon War of 1982, a squad of 12 Israeli paratroopers were up late at night on a border base before crossing over the border into Lebanon the next morning. One of the soldiers was a clairvoyant, and organized a séance for his buddies. They ushered in the soul of their sergeant's grandfather. The soul said, "Tomorrow, you guys will be joining me". One of the soldiers was so scared that he might get killed the next day that he repented and recited psalms all night long, pouring out his heart to Hashem until daybreak. When the sun rose, he broke out with hives and a terrible 104F fever, and was transferred to the infirmary. Without him, his buddies crossed the border the next day, and their armored troop carrier was hit with four RPG shoulder missiles. All eleven died. The twelfth guy was wise enough to escape to Hashem's open arms, and was saved.

Unblemished Innocence

The Torah gives us five wonderful words of advice that guide us on a direct path toward fulfilling the Fifth Principle of emuna while avoiding any ensnarement that misdirects our prayers toward anyone or anything other than Hashem: *Tamim tihyeh im Hashem Elokecha* – "Be wholehearted with Hashem your God" (Deuteronomy 18:13). Our sages and classic elaborators of Torah not only translate but interpret each word of Torah. In our passage at hand, they give a number of significant meanings to the word *tamim*, each a rare gem of advice in serving Hashem. The word I chose in translating this passage – "wholehearted" – is a synthesis of their translations, reflecting the importance of serving the Almighty and praying to Him with all of our hearts.

Rashi, when referring to ritual sacrifices, translates *tamim* as "unblemished" (see Rashi, Leviticus 1:3). Yet, when he translates and interprets our passage at hand, he says: "Walk with Him [Hashem] in innocence and seek Him and not fortune-tellers; accept everything that happens to you with innocence and then you will be with Him and part of Him."

Rashi explains that by walking with Hashem in innocence, appealing to Hashem only without looking for solutions or salvations from astrologers, clairvoyants and the like, and by accepting whatever Hashem does without question, one attains a state of clinging to Hashem and becoming "part of Him", the highest form of perfection a human can attain. This, according to Rashi, is unblemished innocence that is indicative of serving Hashem with a whole heart.

King David's main aspiration in life was the same *tmimus*, or state of unblemished innocence and wholeheartedness, that Rashi's elaboration refers to. King David uses the word *tamim* in several key passages: in Psalm 15:2, he says that the innocent (tamim) individual who acts in justice shall dwell with Hashem. In Psalm 18:24 he prays, "And I shall be wholehearted (tamim) with Him, and I shall be protected from iniquity." The word *tamim* recurs in many other passages of Psalms, showing that the "innocence" that King David aspires to is not at all gullibility but integrity.

Rabbi Chaim ben Attar, the holy "Ohr Hachaim" writes that one attains the level of unblemished innocence when purity of the mouth reflects an equal purity of the heart. In other words, one's prayers should not be lip service or a wolf in sheep's clothing.

The Piasczena Rebbe, Rabbi Klonimus Kalman Shapiro of sacred martyred memory, who before he was murdered by the Nazis in the Holocaust wrote under the direst of circumstances, "Even if you are broken and suffering, yet you strengthen yourself to cling to Hashem in wholehearted, unblemished innocence, because you know that Hashem is with you in your tribulation, you won't seek the future in desperation because you can't see an end to your darkness, but whatever happens to you in life, accept with unblemished innocence and then you will be with Him, and that of course will hasten your salvation" (Aish Kodesh, Parshat Shoftim).

In summarizing the concept of wholeheartedness and unblemished innocence, the Ramban describes the state of purity of heart and wholeness in the service of Hashem when a person prays only to Him and appeals only to Him, no matter what anything others might say (Ramban, Deuteronomy 18:13).

The individual who never makes the mistake of looking to the stars or to the angels for salvation while praying to Hashem only ascends to a level above them. What's more, he or she can rule over them!

Rabbi Alexander Ziskind in his elaboration of Psalm 148 notes that a person in this lowly physical world has the power of commanding all the creations – both in the upper worlds and in the lower worlds – to praise Hashem; they are required to obey, as a fundamental law embedded in the very fiber of creation. Anyone who realizes that his or her prayers, Psalms, and songs of praise have the power to dictate orders to all of creation will surely acquire a burning desire to strengthen this Fifth Principle of emuna and pray exclusively to Hashem, yearning only for Him.

The Sixth Principle: The Words of the Prophets

Principle 6: I believe with complete belief that all the words of the prophets are true.

We believe in the prophecies of all the forty-eight prophets and seven prophetesses mentioned in the *Tanach* and do not doubt that their prophecies are the word of Hashem and therefore truth.

Why is it so critically important to know that the words of the prophets are true?

In our detailed explanation of truth (see Introductory Chapter, "Truth vs. Agenda"), we showed that there is no truth outside the context of Hashem and emuna. Most of what people call truth, or their "personal" truth, is far from absolute truth but rather agenda, tailored to their own expediency and desires.

The Rambam explains that the words of the true prophets, those whose *prophecies* are recorded in the Tanach, come from their direct communication with Hashem

(Rambam, Mishneh Torah, Laws of the Fundamentals of Torah 7:3). We must emphasize that the Rambam states "prophecies" and not "inspirations", for there is a world of difference between the two.

Prophecy, according to the Rambam, is a vision sent directly from Hashem by way of a parable or metaphor that is engraved on the prophet's heart in a way that he understands the message and can convey it to the people it addresses. Simply speaking, this is Hashem communicating directly to the prophet. As Hashem is true and His words are true, so are the prophecies of the true prophets that have been codified in the Tanach. True prophecy can only be Divinely originated.

As opposed to prophecy, inspiration may either originate in the human heart or be Divinely originated. In that respect, a person can claim that his or her inspiration is a Divinely-oriented inspiration, but if they have the slightest trace of self-interest, their inspiration cannot and will not be Divine. For that reason, inspiration cannot be the basis of Torah or Torah law because one never knows the true origin of the inspiration. The false prophecies, which the

Torah so sternly warns against, either speak against explicit Torah commandments or else fail to materialize (See Deuteronomy 13:2-4, 18:20-22). In most cases, the false prophecies are at best personally inspired and always motivated by self-interest and political expedience.

Truth, not Political Correctness

The prophets show us how far we are from truth today. They are our national conscience, prodding us to make teshuva and get close to Hashem. Since the prophecies came directly from Hashem, they were untainted by political correctness and expediency.

To be worthy recipients of direct Divine messages, the prophets were extraordinary in their level of piety, purity and utter self-nullification. Their thoughts, speech and deeds were identically holy; in other words, they spoke and acted in exact accordance to the way they thought. They clung to Hashem, as King David, also a true prophet, testifies, "You, Hashem, are before me always" (Psalm 16:8). Despite the fact that David was King of Israel, he denied himself material amenities, even a good night's sleep, and thought of Hashem and spoke to Him constantly.

The latter kings of Judea and Israel drifted away from Torah and fell into the populism of idolatry. The prophets chastised them and often paid the price of truth with martyrdom.

King Menashe killed Isaiah the Prophet (see Yevamot 49b).

Jeremiah the Prophet prophesized war and the Destruction of the Temple. The false prophets, whom he chastised for placating the populace with prophecies of peace, plotted against him to kill him. His fellow priests, whom he denounced because of their greed, had him tortured and incarcerated.

"And the spirit of Hashem clothed Zachariah the son of Jehoyada the priest; and he stood above the people, and said unto them: 'Thus says God: Why do you transgress the commandments of Hashem, and you shall not succeed; because you have forsaken Hashem, He has also forsaken you.'" Zachariah said this reproof in the Holy Temple on Yom Kippur. King Yoash didn't like it, nor did the priestly authorities. They stoned and killed him then and there, in the Holy Temple on Yom Kippur.

Just as the prophets dedicated themselves to Hashem in a manner that defied nature in their willingness to give their lives for the truth of Hashem's word, Hashem gave them the power to defy nature.

Above Nature and Beyond Logic

Elisha the Prophet, understudy and successor of Elijah the Prophet, repeatedly demonstrated the capability of the true prophet to dictate and overturn nature in a virtually unimaginable manner.

Miracles were the course of nature for Elisha, for he was so bound to Hashem that he barely experienced a material existence. He revived a dead child. He purified the contaminated waters of Jericho which were considered to be a cause of miscarriages and fatalities. When Ovadia's poor widow was threatened with debtors who were about to abduct her two sons, Elisha made a small vial of olive oil flow continuously until it filled enough casks for her to pay off her debts and feed her family. When one of his pupils accidentally dropped an ax into the Jordan River, Elisha made it float on the surface so that he could retrieve it.

Yet, the most moving of Elisha's miracles affected the entire nation, both militarily and economically 9 see Kings II: Ch. 6-7):

The King of Aram waged war against Israel. His strategy to attain a quick and decisive victory involved guerilla tactics and surprise attacks, whose main objective was to ambush the King of Israel and his entourage. Despite precise intel, every one of his surprise attacks were futile. The King of Aram suspected a spy in his inner circle of officers and advisors and interrogated them. They answered in defense of themselves, "No, my lord, O king; but Elisha, the prophet of Israel, tells the king of Israel the words that you speak in your bedroom" (ibid., 6:12).

That same night, the King of Aram sent an entire regiment to kill Elisha. The next morning, Elisha's pupil and attendant awoke before dawn to pray and froze when he looked out the window: the surrounding hills were full of Aramean soldiers and chariots. In utter fear, he cried, "My master, what do we do?"

Elisha told the young man not to fear, for "we have more forces than they do." He prayed to Hashem to enable the pupil to see on a higher spiritual level, and the young man saw that they were protected by chariots of fire with horses of fire. Elisha then prayed that the attacking legion should be blinded. They were. Instead of having the captives killed, he told Yoram to give them bread and water and send them home peacefully to Aram.

Outmaneuvered once more by Elisha, the frustrated Aramean king Ben-Hadad decided to descend upon Samaria with his entire army. As a result, the siege turned a terrible drought that dwindled Israel's food reserves into a horrifying famine, where in accordance with the Torah's curse (see Deuteronomy 28:23), people began to eat their own children. At that time, to stay alive, the populace was eating anything it could get its hands on, kosher or not. Prices were so exorbitant that a donkey's head sold for eighty silver talons and people were sifting pigeon droppings in search for a few undigested grains.

King Yoram of Israel, son of the wicked Ahab and Jezebel, directed his wrath toward Elisha and threatened to kill him. Once again, Elisha knew that an assassin, one of Yoram's senior servants, was on the way and barred the door against him, foiling this plot too.

With starvation rampant and Samaria under siege, Elisha undauntedly challenged Yoram to shun the wicked ways of his parents and to heed the word of Hashem. To prove that Hashem is truth, at the height of the famine and siege, Elisha declared, "Tomorrow at this time shall a measure of fine flour be sold for a shekel, and two measures of barley for a shekel, in the gate of Samaria" (Kings II, 7:1).

King Yoram's military attaché, who stood next to the king when Elisha approached, said sarcastically and in utter disbelief and disrespect, "What, will Hashem create windows in the Heavens and drop down all this grain?"

Elisha responded, "You'll see it but you won't eat from it."

After midnight, Hashem opened the ears of the Arameans and let them hear the uproar of thousands of chariots, trumpets and attack forces. The Aramean soldiers panicked, thinking that the King of Israel hired the legions of the Hittites and the Egyptians to fight against them. They abandoned their entire camp and fled on foot, leaving behind all their equipment, arms and provisions.

The next day in Shomron, the capital city of the Northern Kingdom of Israel, the price of fine flour dropped to a shekel per measure just as Elisha said it would. In the people's rush out of the city gates to collect spoils from the abandoned Aramean camp, the king's military attaché was trampled to death. He saw the spoils but did not partake of them.

Rebbe Akiva and the Fox

Rebbe Akiva had the highest level of belief in the words of the prophets, as the Gemara in Tractate Makkot 24b relates:

Rabban Gamliel, Rabbi Elazar ben Azaria and Rabbi Yehoshua Ben Chanania – the spiritual leaders of the generation - together with Rebbe Akiva travelled to Jerusalem. When they reached Mount Scopus, they rent their clothes, for the Holy Temple had already been destroyed. As they approached the Temple Mount, they saw a fox run out of the innermost chamber, the Holy of Holies. The great wise men wept, but Rebbe Akiva laughed.

"Why are you laughing?" they asked him.

Talmudically, answering a question with a question, Akiva asked, "Why are you crying?"

The great wise men answered, "When foxes run in the place where only the High Priest may enter on Yom Kippur, isn't it befitting that we cry?"

"That is why I laughed," Akiva answered. "I know two prophesies. The first, of the prophet Micah saying, 'Because of you, Zion will be a plowed field. Jerusalem a ruin, and the Temple Mount a forest.' The second, of Zachariah saying, 'Old men and women will yet rejoice in the streets of Jerusalem.' Until I saw the first prophesy fulfilled, I feared the second would never happen. Now that I have seen the first prophesy come true, I *know* the second will materialize also."

The others answered, "Akiva, you have consoled us! Akiva, you have consoled us!" Rebbe Akiva's entire thought process was emuna-oriented; he knew that the word of Hashem as conveyed by our true prophets is truth for posterity.

The Seventh Principle: Moses, the Foremost Prophet

Principle 7: I believe with complete belief that the prophecy of Moses, may he rest in peace, was real, and that he was the foremost of the all the prophets, the ones before him and the ones after him.

We believe that the "Five Books of Moses" – the Torah – was given to Moses from Hashem and that every word is absolute truth. Whereas prophecy was Hashem's way of speaking to the prophets, we believe that Hashem spoke to Moses directly (Exodus 33:11, Deuteronomy 34:10).

In Chapter 12 of the Book of Numbers, the Torah tells how Aaron and Miriam, both prophets in their own right, were talking about their brother Moses, who had discontinued marital intimacy with his wife. "They said, "Has Hashem spoken only to Moses? Hasn't He spoken to us too?" And Hashem heard" (Numbers 12:2).

Aaron and Miriam thought that they were on an equal spiritual footing with their younger brother Moses. After all, they were prophets too! Despite the fact that they meant no harm, for they loved their brother very much, Hashem nonetheless chastised them. Hashem summons Aaron and Miriam to the holy Tent of Meeting. After the Torah remarks that Moses was the humblest man to ever walk the face of the earth, Hashem scolds them as follows:

"Heed My words: if there be a prophet among you, I Hashem shall reveal Myself to him in a vision; I shall speak with him in a dream" (ibid., 6).

But Moses is different. In Hashem's own words, "My servant Moses is trusted in all My house… with him I shall speak mouth to mouth, manifestly and not in riddles; for he beholds the image of Hashem" (ibid., 7-8).

The above passage highlights the difference between Moses and all the other prophets. Their prophecies came to them in a dream or when they were immobilized, lying down in semi-consciousness. In stark contrast, Moses was fully awake and standing on his feet when Hashem spoke to him, as the Torah bears witness: "And when Moses would come before Hashem, so that He could speak with Him, he removed his veil until he came out" (Exodus 34:34). What's more, the other prophets would tremble and look delirious when the spirit of prophecy came to them, as if they were suffering a seizure. Moses, on the other hand, would talk to Hashem like a person would speak to a close friend.

The other prophets lacked the ability to prophesize whenever they wished. Since Moses maintained such a lofty spiritual level, the power of prophecy was continuously at his disposal. This too is documented in the Torah on two occasions, with the pallbearers of Joseph's coffin and the daughters of Slofchod, when Moses must first consult with Hashem before he answers their question. Hashem readily provides Moses with the answers he seeks.

The Validity of Moses as Leader and Prophet

Although Moses performed many remarkable miracles such as splitting the Red Sea and eliciting water from a rock, he did so out of necessity, and not because he wanted to prove his supernatural powers or to validate his status as a prophet. When Moses brought down the manna, the heaven-sent bread, he did so because the nation needed food in the desert. When he sweetened the bitter waters, he did so because the nation was thirsty. The miracles he performed were not the reason that the Nation of Israel accepted him as their valid leader and Hashem's prophet. Hashem's revelation to the Jewish People on Mount Sinai established Moses' status beyond a doubt for posterity.

Whereas all the other religions believe in a revelation of some assumed prophet or holy man who reveals some message that either no other else or only a select inner group of individuals was privy to, 600,000 Jewish males above the age of twenty saw and heard the Almighty reveal Himself on Mount Sinai. Together with their wives and children, there were more than two million witnesses and probably many more than that. Before his death, when Moses implores the Jewish People to observe and uphold the Torah, he says: "Hashem did not make this covenant with our fathers, but with us, all of us, who are all here alive this day" (Deuteronomy 5:3). Again, Moses makes this declaration in front of the whole populace with no one protesting, objecting or taking exception. The entire nation knew that this was a factual account, passed down from parent to child and from teacher to pupil down the unbroken chain of tradition for the last 112 generations since Mount Sinai.

In *Halacha*, Jewish Law, the criteria for acceptable witnesses are very severe. As such, the testimony of two uncontested and approved witnesses in a Court of Jewish Law suffice to establish something as fact. In the case of Mount Sinai, we have 600,000 witnesses. Not a single individual in their generation protested or contested the fact that Hashem revealed Himself to Moses on Mount Sinai in earshot of the entire nation. Hashem says to Moses, as recorded in the Torah: "Behold, I come to you in the midst of a cloud, so that the people may hear when I speak with you, and they shall believe also in you forever" (Exodus 19:9). We see from this amazing passage that Hashem Himself is dictating our Seventh Principle of Emuna, our belief in our teacher Moses and in his leadership and prophecy.

Since the entire People of Israel heard Hashem reveal Himself to Moses at Sinai, Moses needs no further proof of his status.

Were it not for Mount Sinai, one might doubt the veracity of Moses' prophecy based on miracles alone. The agnostics and other skeptics would try to attribute the wonders and miracles that Moses performed as natural coincidence, quirk or witchcraft. Yet, the revelation on Mount Sinai and the hundreds of thousands of witnesses render their claims futile, null and void.

The Importance of the Seventh Principle

Miracles and magic are not the test of the true prophet. True prophecy is the word of Hashem and the Torah is Hashem's law as given to Moses. Therefore, if any self-appointed prophet performs miracles and sound-and-light shows in the horizon, yet contradicts any of the Torah's commandments in the slightest, he is an utter impostor.

The hallmark importance of the Seventh Principle is its emphasis on the firm foundation of Moses' prophecy, witnessed by all of our ancestors in that generation. In a court of religious law, a witness can't come in off the sidewalk and strike down the recorded testimony of two valid witnesses. In like manner, an assumed prophet can't strike down the testimony of hundreds of thousands of witnesses who saw and heard Hashem's revelation to Moses on Mount Sinai. This, as we explained, is not only the basis of the validity of our Torah, but also of Moses' prophecy. As such, miracles, marvels and all sorts of apparent revelations cannot be true if they contradict any of Hashem's commandments in the slightest.

The litmus test of adherence to Hashem's mitzvoth as the prerequisite for true prophecy has been effective throughout the ages in exposing false prophets.

Korach, according to the "Imrei Menachem" of Alexander, was considered a tzaddik, a righteous individual, until he doubted the veracity of Moses' prophecy and led a revolt against Moses' authority. To be called a tzaddik, one must have unblemished emuna, as Habakkuk the Prophet teaches, "The tzaddik shall live by his emuna." Since our Seventh Principle, the belief in the absolute veracity of Moses' prophecy, is an important part of emuna, once Korach denied this, he lost his status as a tzaddik.

Moses answers Korach's rebellion by declaring, "Hereby you shall know that Hashem has sent me to do all these deeds, and that I have not done them of mine own accord" (Numbers 16: 28), followed by the subsequent proof that if Korach and his cronies die a natural death, Moses says, "Then Hashem didn't send me" (ibid., 29). Then and there, the ground opened up miraculously and swallowed Korach, his fellow rebels and their families alive.

In concluding this chapter, we must stress that the Sixth Principle, our overall belief in the true prophets, is insufficient without our Seventh Principle of Emuna. This principle teaches that no prophecy can ever contradict, even in the slightest, the word of Hashem as revealed to Moses, the foremost prophet of all time.

The Eighth Principle: The Unbroken Chain of Torah

Principle 8: I believe with complete belief that the entire Torah we have in our possession today is the one given to Moses, may he rest in peace.

This is the belief in the Divine origin of our Torah, for the Torah we read and learn today is the exact same Torah that Hashem gave to Moses.

The Rambam emphasizes two salient points in this principle: first, "the entire Torah we have in our possession today;" and second, "the one given to Moses."

Principle Eight is a continuation of Principle Seven, where we learned that all of Moses' prophecy is true and directly from the source of truth, the Creator. The Creator gave the entire Torah to Moses. The skeptics ask, "How can this be? Not only the Oral Torah, but even the Prophets and the

Scriptural writing come after Moses!" The answer is very simple, for the truth is simple.

The Written Torah and the Oral Torah

Hashem dictated the Pentateuch to Moses, word for word, which Moses wrote down. As such, the written Torah is also called, the "Five Books of Moses." Yet, the written Torah is more accurately known as the *Tana'ch*, an acronym of *Torah, Nevi'im, Kesuvim*, the Torah, the Prophets and the Scriptural writings. Hashem showed these to Moses as well, although they were written down by prophets who followed Moses. The written Torah ends with the Book of Esther, and nothing can be added after that.

In the Five Books of Moses, Hashem gives 613 commandments, or *mitzvas*, to Moses. Yet, these commandments are presented in telegraphic form, in utter brevity. Hashem therefore explained orally to Moses how to perform each one of these mitzvoth. For example, Hashem commands that we put *mezuzas* on the doorposts of our homes. Were it not for the Oral Torah, Hashem's explanations to Moses, we wouldn't have the slightest idea what a mezuza should look like, how to prepare one, or where exactly to post it.

The same goes for Kosher slaughtering, or *shechitah*. The written Torah commands us to eat only ritually-slaughtered meat with three words, *u'zvachta...ka'asher tzivisicha*, "and you shall slaughter...as I have commanded you." (Deuteronomy 12:21) What is the nature of the command here? We don't see it explicit in the Torah! Rashi explains that these are all the laws of kosher slaughtering as Hashem explained to Moses.

If we want to see Hashem's explanations to Moses, we must refer to the Oral Torah, which includes all the details of fulfilling each mitzvah. At first, the Oral Torah was not to be written, but to be taught orally from father to son and from teacher to pupil just as Hashem taught Moses. Yet during the generation of Rebbe Akiva when the Roman occupation of the Land of Israel and the persecution of the Jews were so terrible, the Oral Torah was in danger of being forgotten.

Codifying the Oral Torah

Rebbe Akiva learned from King David (see Psalm 119:126), that sometimes, one must serve Hashem and preserve His Torah by breaking a Torah ordinance. For example, the oral law states that one may violate a written Torah commandment if it is required to save a life.[3] The Oral Torah was in grave danger of being forgotten, for the sages were pursued and executed, with few surviving. Rebbe Akiva concluded that he must codify the Oral Law, lest it be forgotten, and with it, all of Judaism, Heaven forbid. He therefore assembled a framework of six main categories – the agricultural laws, the special occasions, the laws pertaining to marriage and women, civil law and jurisprudence, Temple rituals, and ritual purity. These became the Six Orders of the Mishna.

After the Romans persecuted and murdered Rebbe Akiva, his student Rebbe Meir polished the language of the Mishna and his student, Rabbi Judah the Prince aka "Rebbe" prepared the final codification of the Mishna.

The Oral Torah and the written Torah are inseparable, as no text can have any authoritative meaning without an accompanying *tradition* as to what it means. Tradition is the key word in Torah. In fact, the Hebrew word for tradition, *mesora*, literally means the consecutive passing of

---

[3] There are three exceptions to this rule: one may not commit idolatry, bloodshed or a forbidden sexual act to save a life (Yerushalmi, tractate Sanhedrin, Ch. 3:5).

both the written Torah and the Oral Torah from generation to generation, just as relay-race runners pass the baton from one to another. This is vital in preserving the exact law of Hashem as given to Moses.

The rationalists of all times protest and claim that the rabbis of the Oral Torah invented nuances of their own initiative. Mesora, our unbroken chain of Torah tradition, proves them utterly wrong.

The Unbroken Chain

In his introduction to the Mishna, the Rambam lists the unbroken chain of Torah tradition from teacher to pupil, documented in each generation. Moses received the Torah, both oral and written, from the Almighty and taught it to his prime student Joshua; Joshua taught the elders. The Elders taught the prophets. The prophet Eli taught Samuel, Samuel taught David, David taught Achiya the Shilonite and Achiya taught Elija.

The last of the prophets – Ezra, Nechemia and Daniel – were the first *Anshei Knesses Hagdolah*, Men of the Great Assembly. The last of them was High Priest Shimon Hatzaddik, who passed the Torah on to Antigones of Socho. Antigones of Socho passed the Torah down to the Tannaim, the sages of the Mishna, the Tannaim on to the Amoraim, the sages of the Gemara, then to the Savuraim, then to the Gaonim, then to the Rishonim, then to the Achronim, which brings us to today.

The pseudo-enlightened, undaunted and unwilling to accept a truth that obligates them, protest, "Why should we accept man-made laws?"

The Torah in our hands today is by no means a set of man-made laws. Just as we explained the unbroken chain of teacher to pupil, we can see the unbroken chain of the Torah's law, from the word of Hashem as given to Moses all the way down to the rabbi of your community today.

As mentioned previously, since the Oral Law was in danger of being forgotten, it was written down and codified in the Mishna. Yet, the Mishna is written in telegraphic form so that it is readily committed to memory. The Gemara therefore comes to clarify the Mishna, explain it in greater detail and determine the *halacha*, or applicable law. The Savuraim explain the Talmud further while the Gaonim enhanced Talmudic scholarship and spread its teachings. The Sephardi Rishonim, such as the Rambam (Maimonides), the Ri'f (Rabbi Yitzchak Elfasi) and the Ro'sh (Rabbenu Asher) composed Halachic compendia of the Talmud while the Ashkenazi Rishonim such as Rashi and the Tosefot elaborated on the Talmud while citing the practical halachas within the body of their elaborations.

Seeing the toll that poverty and persecution took on Jewry after the Spanish Inquisition, one of the first Sephardi Achronim, Rabbi Joseph Caro, took the teachings of the Rambam, the Ri'f and the Ro'sh and boiled them down into a single Code of Jewish Law, the *Shulchan Aruch*. One of the first Ashkenazi Achronim, Rabbi Moshe Isserles aka the "Ram'a", highlights those halachas where Ashkenazi custom and practice differs from the Sephardi.

To this day, our Rabbinical scholars continue to elaborate on Halacha and apply it to the type of modern-day situations and technology that our ancestors didn't have to deal with.

We stress again the Halachic nuances are not "new manmade inventions" but rather the practical application of Mosaic

Law that can never go out of style and never be antiquated, since it was given to Moses by the Creator; since He is eternal, so is His Torah. Just as the Creator is relevant, for He is responsible for every heartbeat and every breath we take, so is His Torah, which is the exact Torah that we have in our hands today.

The Opposing Schools of Moses and Korach

Rabbi Yitzchok Zev Soloveitchik, the "Brisker Rov" writes that Korach denied two of the principles of emuna, the seventh and the eighth: he couldn't accept that Moses' prophecy was true and he didn't believe that the Torah came straight from Hashem. Korach's agnosticism and his obstinacy cost him his life, as we explained in the beginning of this chapter.

Let's take a closer look at the opposing schools of thought of Moses and Korach. This in itself is more testimony of Torah's timeliness, for the episode of Korach's rebellion against Moses, which is none other than a rebellion against Hashem and His Torah, is still with us today. Three main differences characterize the stark contrast between Moses and Korach:

1. Self-Interest: Moses was devoid of self-interest, to the extent that he testifies to Hashem, "I have not taken a single donkey from the populace, neither have I hurt any of them." (Numbers 16:15). Korach, on the other hand, was motivated by his desire for money and power in general and particularly to become leader of the Levites. Whereas Moses was the humblest human ever, Korach clothed himself in arrogance.

2. Logic: Moses cast all logic aside in nullifying himself to the Creator; Korach refused to accept anything the countered his rationale and logic. For example, Korach would say, "Who needs a mezuza with two tiny paragraphs of Torah written in it on the doorpost of my house when I have a wall full of Torah books at home!" Korach forgets one thing, that the mezuza is a commandment from the Almighty that is not based on any human rationale or logic. Consequently, in denying the mitzva, he denies Hashem and His Torah.

3. Nature: Moses paid no attention to nature and its limitations. His emuna in Hashem, characterized by his incessant prayers, governed his thought, speech and deeds. Korach contrastingly tried to accomplish his goals by natural means –

greed, lobbying and even rebelling even though it entailed violating Hashem's commandments.

An example of the contemporary Korach is in the prohibition of pork. The School of Korach, who doesn't want to be limited to kosher food and kosher restaurants says, "In the time of Moses, there was no sanitary means of slaughter and pork suffered from Trichinosis (roundworm), so pork had to be outlawed for health reasons. But today, with modern means of processing, there is no more Trichinosis and no need to prohibit pork." Wrong on two counts. There still is trichinosis, but that's not the reason we don't eat pork. Hashem commanded us to refrain from eating pork. Self-interest, logic or nature has nothing to do with it.

Although we neither look for logic in Hashem's commandments nor base our observance on logic, the Zohar and Kabbalah often mention the underlying spiritual rationale of a mitzva. Hashem, as Creator of the human soul knows what's best for the human soul. The Zohar says that one who eats the flesh of swine enclothes his or her soul in the impure spirit of that animal, which blocks Divine light and subdues any and all desire for holiness. In other words, by eating pork, one distances himself from Hashem, Heaven forbid, which is the exact opposite of what he should be striving for in his world. Namely, getting close to Hashem.

In concluding Principle Eight, the Rambam explains that every word of Torah has deep secrets to those who understand them. Many of these secrets are revealed in gematria, or numerical equivalents of each letter that comprises a given word or phrase, in acronyms or in many other different ways, such as examining every other letter, every third letter and so forth.

Here's one small example. The Yerushalmi Talmud in Chapter 3 of Tractate Avoda Zara mentions casually that the world is round and our sages in the time of Alexander the Great, over 2300 years ago, knew that the world was round. In the Book of Genesis, the Creator often reveals himself as "Sha-dai", spelled shin, dalet, yud. The numerical sum of these three letters is 314. 314, divided by 100 – the number that's indicative of perfection – is 3.14, or Pi! Pi is the secret of the circle, for without it, one cannot compute the area of a circle or its circumference. What's more, as Pi is the square root of ten, indicative of the ten spheres of Godliness, it's an infinite number just like the source of the ten spheres, the Creator.

Now that we've learned that all the Torah we have in our possession today is the one given to Moses, we'll now learn, with Hashem's help, our next principle that the Torah is for posterity, never to be replaced.

The Ninth Principle: The Eternal Torah

Principle 9: I believe with complete belief that this is the Torah, it shall not be replaced nor will the Creator blessed be His Name give us a different Torah.

This is the belief that the Torah we have today is the Torah we have for posterity, unchangeable and irreplaceable, relevant for posterity.

The holy Zohar says in several places that Hashem looked in the Torah and created the world. King David alludes to this when he says, "Before the mountains were created..." (Psalm 90:2). Our sages teach that Hashem wrote his Torah 974 generations before creation, and ultimately, the Torah became the blueprint He used to create the world.

As we have already learned extensively throughout our previous principles of emuna, Hashem is truth and His Torah is truth. Since the entire universe and everything in it from the greatest macro to the tiniest micro was created according to Hashem's Torah, if the Torah would be

114

rescinded or replaced, the world would cease to exist. The Torah is not only the blueprint of creation, but the sustenance of creation as well.

Since Torah is the blueprint of creation, all the underlying wisdom of creation for posterity can be found in the Torah. One shining example is the discovery of vaccines and immunization.

Louis Pasteur and the Wisdom of Torah

French scientist Louis Pasteur (1822-95) – known as "the father of microbiology" – was famous for his revolutionary findings in the causes and prevention of disease. He created the first vaccines for rabies and anthrax. His best-known innovation was "pasteurization," his heat-treatment method for preventing bacterial contamination in milk and wine.

Pasteur owes his monumental development of vaccines to Talmudic knowledge, which, over fifteen centuries before he was born, describes how administering a weak form of a disease to humans could cause immunity to its virulent version.

Rabbi Dr. Israel Michel Rabinowitz (1818-93) was a scion of a distinguished family of rabbis and Talmudic scholars. He himself was an ordained rabbi who studied in the best Lithuanian yeshivas before he went to Paris to pursue medical studies. Although he earned his M.D. in 1865, he never practiced medicine. Instead, he embarked on a project to translate the Talmud into French.

While living in Paris, Rabbi Dr, Rabinowitz became close friends with Louis Pasteur, to whom he showed some of his Talmudic translations, especially those that deal with science and medicine.

One particular Talmudic discussion Tractate Yoma 83b grabbed Pasteur's attention. There, our sages give the five signs of a rabid dog: open mouth, dripping saliva, tail between its legs, abnormal gait, and droopy ears. What even more fascinated Pasteur was the Talmudic cure for rabies: the Gemara states, "If someone was bitten by a rabid dog, one should feed him the lobe of that dog's liver." Although dog liver of course is not kosher, it may be used as a cure to save a life as in the case of rabies, which is often fatal, Heaven forbid.

From the Talmud's wisdom in the case of the rabid dog, Pasteur concluded that one could cure infectious ailments by introducing small amounts of an infection into a body – avian, animal or human – and that the infected body would produce antibodies that could fight a major onslaught of the same infectious organism. He tested his theory by subjecting chickens to a mild form of cholera; they in turn developed immunity to cholera.

Pasteur went on to successfully create cholera, anthrax, and rabies vaccines, which paved the way for many additional vaccines, all thanks to the timeless wisdom of Torah. As the blueprint to the world, the Torah is also the source of sustenance for the world. As such, it will never be rescinded or replaced.

No Additions, No Detractions

The Rambam stresses that by virtue of the Torah's Divine origin, for it was all given to Moses on Mount Sinai (as we learned in Principle Eight), nothing may be added and nothing may be detracted, not from the written Torah nor from the Oral Torah.

Rebbe Yitzchak Isaac Yehuda Yechiel Safran (1806-1874), the Komarna Rebbe and a brilliant scholar in both the revealed and esoteric sides of Torah, writes in his elaboration of the Pentateuch (Heichal Bracha, Parshas Breishis): "The Rambam in his holy tongue teaches that our Torah comes directly from the Creator blessed be He and not from anyone else, and we may therefore neither add nor detract from the written Torah or from the Oral Torah, for the Torah itself commands (Deuteronomy 13:1), 'And you shall neither add nor detract from her [the Torah]'...

"We learned in the Eighth Principle that Moses did not add or detract a single word of Torah, whether in reference to Divine holiness or the mundane, including 'Timna was Lotan's sister' etc. and that the entire Oral Torah was also given to Moses, which he passed down from mouth to mouth and from generation to generation.

"The entire Torah will not be replaced nor rescinded for in essence, it is all our belief that it is an assemblage of Hashem's Names where each letter is a Divine light that will never be replaced, nor will its order be altered – the beginning won't move to the end and the end won't move to the beginning. There will not be a new Torah from the Creator nor a change in our Torah.

Yet, in the future, more of the Torah's inner secrets shall be revealed as we await the fulfillment of the prophecy when the entire world shall fill with spiritual awareness."

In light of the above, if someone comes along with the claim of a new Torah or a new prophecy, we neither believe it nor accept it. Judaism never accepted Christianity's false claims, since their new testament denies and condemns many laws of Torah while adding a false notion that one must believe in and worship a flesh-and-blood savior in order to attain salvation. What's more, the Christian "prophecy" comes more than 500 years after Esther and Mordechai, the last prophets.

The same goes for Islam and the Koran. Mohammed's "prophecy" was a nuance of 7th Century CE.

Both Christianity and Islam often reverted to the sword throughout history to "convince" the Jews to fall in line with their nuances, which trample our Ninth Principle of Emuna. Moses did not have to convince the Jewish People that he was Hashem's prophet, because they all heard Hashem speak to him when they stood at Mount Sinai.

No Tricks, No Shticks

The Rambam also has Christianity and Islam in mind when writes, "If a person arises, whether from Israel or from the nations, and performs some wonder or miracle and claims that Hashem sent him to add or detract a commandment of Torah, or interprets the Torah in a manner that contradicts the prophecy of Moses, or tells us that a commandment of the Torah is not eternal but antiquated and no longer relevant, then he is none other than a false prophet (Foundations of Torah 9:1)."

A person could come along and perform a sound-and-light show with his fingertips serving as projectors. Another comes along and walks on water. A third does some other trick, like pulling a rabbit out of a hat. Such phenomena could be possible, resulting from magic tricks, sorcery or even manipulation of Divine Names. Yet, no trick or *shtick* (Yiddish slang for "gimmick"), no matter how impressive and supernatural it may appear is proof of prophecy. Indeed, if the performer denies a single letter of Torah, adds or detracts a commandment, he is a false prophet in whom we don't believe.

False and Famous

This generation has been plagued with so-called "kabbalists" and "rebbes" who claim to be privy to the deepest secrets of esoteric Torah. The common denominator between them is that they lack a *mesora*, and neither have the tradition of generation-to-generation nor ordination by and approbation of the generation's Torah leaders. The proof of their utter lack of authenticity is when they tell someone to do something that violates Torah. Rebbe Nathan of Breslev writes that these false leaders, as popular or as sought-after as they may be, are nonetheless rooted in the false prophets and the soothsayers for they purvey false beliefs (Likutei Halachot, Hilchot Chol Hamoed 4:4).

The "false and famous" can be difficult to recognize if someone gives importance to the masses who follow them, often zealously. Yet, a look at them in light of halacha exposes their bogus nature. Maybe they tell their followers to perform an act of violence against those who oppose them. Or maybe they say something improper, much less lay a finger on a woman, in the name of correcting her soul. Or maybe the false and famous pseudo-kabbalist or counterfeit-rebbe tells an individual that he or she doesn't need to repent if they give him a certain sum of money. These are all giveaways revealing the false nature of any given "spiritual guide", for there cannot be any truth in even an iota's deviation from Torah law.

Moshiach and Posterity

People often ask what the Torah's status will be once Moshiach comes. The Rambam, when explaining the laws of the Megilla, makes this statement: "The Megilla of Esther exists just as the Pentateuch and the laws of the Oral Torah, which shall never be nullified" (Laws of Megilla, 2:18).

Moshiach will elaborate on the Torah and spread the knowledge and awareness of Torah, all according to the unbroken tradition passed down by Moses that we discussed earlier in the Eighth Principle. He will fulfill the prophecy, "For the earth shall fill with the knowledge of Hashem, as the waters cover the sea" (Isaiah 11:9). Since we get to know Hashem and attain spiritual awareness only by way of the light of Torah, the Torah never changes just as Hashem never changes. And, just as Hashem is eternal, so is the Torah. The Torah therefore describes itself in at least ten different passages, "Eternal law for all your generations" (Exodus 12:17, Leviticus 23:14, Numbers 16:16 and more).

The Torah is very economical with words. Why then is the Torah redundant, saying both "eternal law" and "for all your generations"? Aren't they both indicative of posterity? The answer is that no generation can say that the Torah is irrelevant, Heaven forbid – not the generation of high-tech and not the generation of Moshiach. A person who claims to be Moshiach, yet comes along with a new Torah that he claims Hashem revealed to him, is certainly not the genuine Messiah. The Torah we have today is the one that was given to Moses, the one that we'll continue to observe when Moshiach comes and the one we'll have forever.

The wonderful aspect of Moshiach that we so look forward to according to Rabbi Yitzchok Zev Soloveitchik, the "Brisker Rov," is that Moshiach will clarify Torah in such a way that it will be as if each of us learned from Elijah the Prophet, as the prophet foresees, "Behold, I send you Elijah the Prophet before the great and awesome day of Hashem" (Malachi 3:23), when we see with our own eyes Hashem's return to

His rebuilt Holy Temple in Jerusalem, speedily and in our days, amen!

The Tenth Principle: Omniscience and Divine Providence

Principle 10: I believe with complete belief that the Creator blessed be His Name knows all the actions of every human and all their thoughts, as it is said, "He produces the hearts of them all and discerns all their doings" (Psalm 33:15).

This is the belief in Hashem's omniscience. Since His Divine Providence determines everything, no thought, utterance or occurrence in the universe is unknown to Him.

The GPS

To explain how Hashem's omniscience works together with His Divine Providence, imagine that Hashem is the GPS in your car, showing you the way to your destination. In fact, the Tenth Principle could accurately be called the "GPS" principle, since it is G'od's P'ersonal S'upervision of each of our lives and all of creation.

This particular GPS is quite advanced; it knows everything that's occurring on the road between your point of embarkation and your destination. When calculating your route, it takes everything into consideration. It's aware of every factor that might affect your trip in any way. This GPS knows where the radar traps are and where every hole in the road is. It sees where the traffic jams are and where the open roads are. But more than that: it sees where another driver is paying attention to an incoming text message and not to the road. It also takes into account your thoughts and state of mind.

We're not finished yet. The GPS, while taking you on your route, has calculated ways that have avoided nails on the road, potential hazards, j-walking pedestrians and all types of perils that would have ruined your trip, your day or even your health and future. Most of the time, you're not even aware of the wonderful service that your GPS has done for you, and you take it for granted, especially if it's a routine trip like to and back from your home to work.

What's more, sometimes you're angry at your GPS and you yell at it: "Why did you take me on 495 instead of my usual route home on 295?!?" If you're fortunate, you hear later on the news that a semi-trailer and a bus were involved in a terrible collision on 295 at the exact time you would have been there. Then, you're really ashamed that you doubted your GPS and yelled at it.

This GPS is a magnificent model. If your body doesn't have enough fluid, it will send a thirst message to your throat so that you'll drink water. If your body needs Vitamin C, the GPS will make you yearn for a fresh tangerine or a glass of fresh-squeezed orange juice. The list of the G'odly P'ersonal S'upervision functions in our lives is endless.

The Manufacturer

The Tenth Principle teaches us that Hashem is much more than the GPS in our lives; He's also our manufacturer. He made each one of us, inside and out! For that reason, when the Rambam states the Tenth Principle, he supports this tenet with a quote from King David: "He produces the hearts of them all and discerns all their doings" (Psalm 33:15). Hashem produces both dimensions of a creation, the manifest physical side known as the body and the invisible spiritual side known as the soul. Every creation on all four levels of creation – mineral, plant, animal and human – has a physical side and a spiritual side, as we explained in the introductory chapter. Since Hashem created both sides of the creation, He knows everything about that creation, not only what it is doing but what it is thinking and feeling.

Technology and Divine Providence

The "Chofetz Chaim", Rabbi Yisroel Meir Kagan of Radin (1838-1933) wrote in his day that the purpose of technological advances is to strengthen our belief in Divine Providence (see Shem Olam, *Hashmatos* at the end). The telescope teaches us that Hashem's universe in macro is far vaster that the naked eye can see. The microscope shows that each creation in micro is far more intricate that the naked eye can realize. Hashem creates the eye that sees and the ear that hears.

At this point, King David chastises all the wicked people who think that they can get away unscathed after hurting, robbing and exploiting people, as if no one knows what they're doing. He says, "Fools, when will you understand? He Who creates the ear, shall He not hear? He who forms the eye, shall He not see?" Hashem's hearing and sight record everything everywhere, better than any search engine on the web and better than the most sophisticated surveillance system. A satellite surveillance camera and Google Search record and document knowledge, but only where they are looking. Neither one knows everything going on in the world, much less in real time. Only Hashem does. But unlike technology, which is sorely limited, Hashem is not, for He is omniscient. "The eyes of Hashem cruise the entire earth" (Zachariah 4:10). "His eyes are open to all the ways of man" (Jeremiah 32:19). "The Guardian of Israel never sleeps or slumbers" (Psalm 121:4).

The closer we get to Moshiach, the more Hashem enables revelations of technology in order to help us realize the concepts of omniscience and Divine Providence. By observing the creations, we learn more about the Creator. In fact, Rebbe Nachman of Breslev begins his magnum opus by obligating each of us to search for the underlying Divine wisdom in each creation (see Likutei Moharan I:1). An Intel I7 computer processor in its use of multithreading technology helps us realize the intricacy of the human brain. Yet, the human operating system is actually stronger, more durable and much more effective than the best of today's computer operating systems, which are really not much more than electronic pack mules. Algorithms make it appear as if search engines and social media forums can think, but they are simply guideline laws for how to stack the electronic packs of data on the backs of the electronic mules. Only humans can reason, and the power of human reason comes from the soul, which is a tiny spark of the Divine.

Although the purpose of technology, as the Chofetz Chaim teaches, is to help us realize how vast Hashem is and how infinite His omniscience and constant Divine Providence are, Hosea the Prophet reminds us that, "The ways of Hashem are just; the righteous walk in them, but the transgressors stumble on them."

When the righteous look at technology, they are awed and humbled, saying, "If the new Capella-2 Synthetic Aperture Radar (SAR) Satellite Spy Camera can penetrate walls to take pictures of a teacup from hundreds of miles in space, and it's only a creation, then imagine what the Creator can do!" The righteous person now can fully internalize the Mishna that says, "An eye sees, an ear hears, and all your deeds are recorded in a book" (Tractate Avos 2:1).

Neither Google Search nor Capella Space can make that claim.

But, like Hosea the Prophet warns, the transgressors stumble on their technological feats to think that they run the world. They create media outlets and corporations that are more powerful than governments and use them to wield power and to attempt to uproot Torah values. They do everything in their power to paint the Torah and her loyal observers as primitive and antiquated, while crowning themselves as the enlightened. Nevertheless, they are just as inane as those who built the tower of Babel some 3,800 years ago. It is therefore no small coincidence that the global leader of Hi-Tech is also the global trend-setter of moral decadence whose social and economic structure are in severe decline.

Like everything else in creation, Hashem gives us technology, but it's our free choice to use it productively and responsibly.

To help us internalize the Tenth Principle and fuel our emuna, we'll conclude this chapter with two stories about Divine Providence.

Scarface

A distraught young man whose face was terribly scarred met with Rav Chaim Kanievski shlit'a. Despite the fact that he was one of the best boys in his Yeshiva, he complained that he never had a second date with a girl, for every girl who looked at him was horrified.

Rav Chaim listened to him patiently and gave him a blessing that his next *shidduch* date should be more fruitful. "Tell the next girl you go out with how you got those scars," he advised.

"Rebbe, what do you mean? I should right away call attention to my scarred face? She's sure to run away!" protested the young man.

Rav Kanievski reassured the young man, who heeded the rabbi's advice. On the next date, before talking about anything else, he told the young lady that he must explain something.

"Do you remember a few years ago during the Intifada in Jerusalem, when Arabs were on a stabbing rampage? Well, I was walking home from yeshiva in the Old City and I heard a terrible scream. Although I'm no fighter or hero, I ran in the direction of the scream and found an Arab wielding a knife in the face of a terrified young Jewish girl. I let out a war-cry, shouting at the Arab to let the girl go and without thinking, I jumped on him. Meanwhile, she ran away, but the Arab slashed my face several times with his knife. I fought him with all my strength until he too ran away. He could have killed me but Hashem didn't let that happen…"

The young man took a deep breath and continued his narrative, "I tried all kinds of surgery to get rid of the scars but nothing helped. I know that my face is ugly and scary, but I think it made it worse."

"I know that I am horrible to look at, but Rav Chaim Kanievski told me to tell the next girl I meet how I got these scars."

The girl's lips quivered and then she burst out in tears.

Visibly upset, the young man asked, "Why are you crying?"

"I was that young girl!" she cried out through her tears, "You saved my life." She looked at him, but saw no scars; she saw her heroic *bashert*, her intended partner for life.

The above story shows us how Hashem's Divine Providence so profoundly governs not only the milestones of our lives but every tiny detail in life, especially in bringing two soul-mates together.

The Malfunctioning Red-Alert Siren

My hometown of Ashdod on the southern coast of Israel has often been the target of terrorist-rocket fire from Gaza, a dozen miles to the south of us. The Red-Alert Alarm system is capable of sensing a rocket as it is fired, then sounds an alarm giving us about 34 seconds to run to shelter (in Ashkelon, it's only 20 seconds to shelter and in Sderot, only 15). The alarm system has been 99% effective. This is a story which many of us here witnessed about one of the lone times when the siren malfunctioned.

The Port Authority of Ashdod erected a concrete igloo on the pier that is capable of sheltering about thirty or so longshoremen during a missile attack, for the bomb shelters are further away from the pier near the warehouses. At any rate, a deadly barrage of rockets was fired in the direction of Ashdod port. The siren failed to go off and the longshoremen continued operating their cranes and forklifts, unloading containers from incoming cargo ships, business as usual...

Two rockets landed at sea but a deadly third one with an upgraded Iranian warhead succeeded in smashing through the concrete roof of the igloo and exploded inside. The walls of the igloo absorbed all the lethal shrapnel and not a single port worker suffered the slightest scratch.

Had the alarm siren functioned normally, all the workers would have made a beeline to the igloo shelter. The malfunction, a product of Hashem's magnificent Divine Providence that predominated over the sophisticated alert system, saved several dozen lives that day. If our flesh-and-blood eyes could see the number of lethal bacteria and viruses lurking in the air all around us, we'd realize that Hashem's magnificent Divine Providence is preserving our lives every moment of the day.

The Eleventh Principle: Reward, Punishment and Free Choice

Principle 11: I believe with complete belief that the Creator blessed be His Name rewards those who observe His commandments and punishes those transgress His commandments.

This is our belief in reward and punishment as well as our belief in mankind's free will to do good or evil, for there can be no concept of reward and punishment outside the context of free will, if there is the slightest coercion in either direction.

To Build or Destroy

The "Ramchal" teaches that there cannot be reward or punishment outside the context of free choice. Furthermore, there is free choice on every spiritual level. It doesn't matter whether a person is the greatest Torah sage or the simplest human on earth; each has free choice on his or her own level. In his classic Kabbalistic book, "136 Openings of Wisdom", he refers to observing a commandment as a *tikkun*, which means both building and rectifying, yet refers to transgressing a commandment as *kilkul*, which means a ruination. According to this eye-opening principle, one who observes a commandment both builds and rectifies the world while the transgressor destroys it (see 136 Openings of Wisdom, Opening 62).

In light of the above teaching, a soul is sent down here to this world to perform a task. When it fulfills what it is meant to do by observing the laws of the Creator, it rectifies, builds and maintains the world. This is easy to understand since the Torah is the Creator's book of laws and the blueprint He used to create the world. To build properly, a builder must follow the master architect's blueprint. Consequently, one who observes a law of Torah creates a *tikkun*, a rectification or a constructive act.

The world is meant to function optimally according to the laws of Torah. Therefore, when a soul transgresses the laws of Torah, something in the world malfunctions. The transgression creates a *kilkul*, a breakdown or a ruination.

Reward and Punishment

Every tikkun comes with a reward while every kilkul brings a punishment. That's understandable, for one who builds, maintains and enhances the Creator's universe deserves a reward while one who destroys it bears liability and is therefore punished. Rabbi Shlomo Elyashiv (1841-1926), also known as the "Ba'al HaLeshem", writes that punishment is not vengeance or vindictiveness, but a cleansing of the soul that enables it to enjoy a blissful hereafter.

Some people erroneously think that either Hashem forgot about their transgressions when they see that despite their evil doings, a bolt of lightning doesn't come from the sky and strike them in the head. The Gemara says, "Anyone who thinks that Hashem has forgotten about their wrongdoings can forget about their life" (Bava Kama 50a). The only thing that can wipe a person's slate clean is *teshuva*, or penitence, which is capable of rectifying any wrongdoing, as long as a person doesn't say, "OK, I'll do a misdeed today and then repent for it tomorrow."

Other religions believe that a person can sin with no worry as long as he or she believes in a flesh-and-blood savior who atones for them. Not so in Judaism! In Chapter Four of "Path of the Righteous" (*Mesillas Yesharim*), The Ramchal reminds us that Hashem judges every act or every person in absolute justice. A person is liable for everything he or she does, and there are no surrogates when it comes to punishment.

One might ask why he or she should be held responsible for what they do when we learned in the First Principle that He alone did, does and will do everything. The Chofetz Chaim answers in Chapter 17 of "Ahavas Chesed" that true, the outcome of a deed is solely up to Hashem, but the desire to do good or evil is up to us, as we will learn later in this chapter. Consequently, one is rewarded for good desires and punished for evil desires.

Reward and punishment are rarely immediate, for if it were, humans would be conditioned like white mice in a laboratory to do what's needed to earn a chunk of cheese or to avoid whatever it must to stay away from something painful. Nevertheless, righteous deeds have immediate effects on the health of the soul while transgressions block Divine light and cause darkness and a concealment of Divine light to the soul.

Cause and Effect

Let's compare the Torah to the owner's manual that comes with a new car showing how to properly maintain that particular model. It states what type of fuel to use and what viscosity of oil to lubricate the car with. It says how much air one should fill the tires with and how often to change oil, put in new spark plugs and bring the car in to an authorized garage for periodic maintenance. The manufacturer always specifies that new-car warranty depends on proper maintenance as detailed in the owner's manual, which was carefully written by the designer of the car.

Imagine that the new car owner wants to save money; instead of using good quality motor oil that would cost about $6.00 a quart, he tries to lubricate his car with a quart of vegetable oil that's on sale at the supermarket for $1.25; he does the same with the fuel, substituting expensive high-octane gasoline that the owner's manual prescribes with diesel fuel that costs half the price. It won't be long before the car gets towed into the garage. The inane owner will not have a legitimate claim that the car doesn't function and will therefore lose all privileges of the warranty.

Don't think for a moment that this is a simple child's parable; it's straight out of the Torah: "Behold, I place before you today a blessing and a curse; the blessing, if you shall heed the commandments of Hashem your God, which I command you today; and the curse, if you shall not heed the commandments of Hashem your God, and stray from the path which I command you today" (Deuteronomy 11:26-28).

The above three passages are especially significant in that they make a simple cause-and-effect statement, as Rabbenu Bachiya writes in his elaboration of the Torah. Whereas heeding a commandment invokes a blessing, transgressing a commandment invokes a curse. Again, one builds or one destroys. This too is simple to understand: if one immerses a hand in cold water, the hand will feel a sensation of cold. If one foolishly places a hand in a fire, the hand will be burned, Heaven forbid.

Our sages teach us throughout the Talmud that coercion exempts a person for punishment. No one deserves to be punished for a transgression they were forced to commit. Likewise, no one deserves a reward for a mitzva that he or she is forced to do at gunpoint. Reward and punishment only make sense in a context of absolute free choice; therefore, the Creator maintains a perfect balance of good and evil in the world so that a person won't be coerced in the slightest in either direction.

Spiritual Anatomy – Where Body Meets Soul

In order to understand reward and punishment, we must understand how body and soul interact and how this interaction determines one's free choice.

There are three levels of the soul that correspond to three levels of the body. Although all three levels of body and soul are vital, we view them vertically, from top to bottom.

The top level is the *neshama*, the Divine soul, which is housed deep inside the brain, its corresponding physical element. Here are one's powers of cognizance and understanding.

The middle level of the soul is *ruach*, the spirit, housed in heart. Within the *ruach* are not only one's power of speech, which separates humanity from the animal kingdom, but a person's desires. These include one's emotions, like love and hate, one's preferences and one's aspirations.

The bottom level of the soul is the *nefesh*, the basic animal soul, which is housed in the liver of a person. *Nefesh* has the strongest connection to the body, for it permeates the blood and operates all of a person's actions and bodily functions. *Nefesh* cannot perform any voluntary action without directives from *ruach* and *neshama*, desire and cognizance.

My esteemed teacher the Melitzer Rebbe shlit'a explains a teaching from the Zohar in Parshas Pinchas that teaches us a profound secret about the interaction of the three levels of the soul. This is the key to understanding the notion of free choice and also explains how a person makes his or her decisions. There are two types of flows between the three vertical levels: the noble flow (top to bottom) and the ignoble flow (bottom to top).

The Noble Flow

The "noble flow" of a decision or choice making process is the flow from top to bottom. It works as follows:

1. The *neshama*, the Divine soul in the brain, clarifies the truth and determines the upright course of action or speech. It passes its conclusion down to *ruach* in the right side of the heart.

2. *Ruach*, the human soul in the right side of the heart, accepts the decision of the *neshama* and converts it into an upright desire. This desire is then converted down downward as a directive to the *nefesh*.

3. *Nefesh*, the animal soul in the liver, is like a horse with a mind of its own. Yet, the strength of a clear directive from *ruach* bridles it so that it leads the physical limbs to perform the desired act.

The result of the noble flow is the performance of a good deed or speech utterance, when *nefesh* takes action according to the directive from *ruach*, whose desire is dictated by the truth clarification of *neshama* above.

In the noble flow, one attains a status of spiritual nobility when one's choices are the outcome of the brain dictates to the heart. This way, the heart's desires, aspirations, likes and dislikes develop in accordance with the spiritual-cognizance that the Divine soul imparts on the brain. Continuing the downward flow of influence from the heart to the liver, the limbs now act accordingly to the spiritually cognizant desires of the heart. This is the proper flow of influence, from top to bottom, which enables a person to emulate the Creator, who is King of kings. As such, we call it the "noble flow".

The Torah states explicitly, albeit in telegraphic manner, when it says in Deuteronomy 4:39, "And you shall know this day, and internalize it in your heart, that Hashem is God in heaven above and upon the earth beneath; there is none else." First, we must learn this knowledge, the knowledge of emuna; then, we must house it firmly in our brain and then bring it down to our heart. Once that's accomplished, the body will act in the most remarkably noble manner imaginable and the individual will enjoy happiness, inner peace and indescribable emotional health. That is the whole purpose of our emphasis on learning the Thirteen Principles of Emuna in such a thorough manner. There is no better path to a truly good life.

The above dynamics from top to bottom enable a human to attain the highest order of true dignity and nobility. They require that the flow of influence be in the correct order that the Creator intended, from *neshama* and brain to *ruach* and heart and then down to *nefesh* and the liver. But, if the flow goes in reverse, from bottom to top, a person enters a self-destruct mode, because he or she is using body and soul in a manner totally contrary to the "Body-Soul Owner's Manual" – the Torah, which was given to us by the body and soul's Creator and Manufacturer, Who knows what's best for it.

The Ignoble Flow

Look what happens when the order of the flow of influence is reverse. When *nefesh* – the basic animal soul housed in the liver – is not restrained and guided, then the body acts like a wild horse that refuses to be controlled. The palate demands certain foods whether or not they're kosher or healthful. The reproductive organs demand pleasures, whether or not they're permissible or moral. The wild bucking-bronco body is much stronger than the heart and easily overcomes it. The animal soul now forces the human soul in the heart to adopt bodily desires, lusts and appetites, ethical or not. The heart will now seek money and pleasure rather than morality and propriety. The heart, vanquished by the body, is liable to desire all types of addictive and adverse substances and behaviors. The delicate *neshama* in the brain is no match for a heart that has fallen captive to the wild desires of the animal *nefesh* in the liver.

Let's summarize the ignoble flow:

The "ignoble flow" of a decision or choice making process is the flow from bottom to top, as follows:

1. Lacking restraint from above, *Nefesh*, the animal soul in the liver, is like a horse with a mind of its own. Unbridled, it leads the physical limbs to perform according to its powerful appetites and bodily drives.

2. *Ruach*, the human soul, succumbs to the bodily drives of *nefesh* and develops animal-like desires, the opposite of holiness and righteousness. This neutralizes *ruach* in the right side of the heart and activates the evil inclination in the left side of the heart. As *ruach* on the right side is deactivated, the evil inclination in the left side of the heart

now dictates desires. This desire is then transferred upward to the brain. *Neshama*, the Divine soul, rather than being subdued leaves altogether, creating a vacuum in the brain that is quickly filled by human logic and intellect.

The ignoble flow renders a person under complete influence of body. In the absence of *ruach* and *neshama*, the human soul and the Divine soul, the brain creates decisions, choices and ideologies that will never conflict with the body's desires and convince itself that it is enlightened. Yet, if and when such "enlightened" individuals lose the fear of being caught in a crime, they will do anything the body dictates. This explains why so many national leaders and politicians who work so hard to climb to the top often exhibit the most ignoble behavior.

The slang of literally every language on earth calls a wild, crass, rude and coarse individual an *animal*. This is rightfully so, for such a person's human soul in the right side of the heart has succumbed to the evil inclination in the left side of the heart and its base animal desires.

The Challenge of Free Choice

This lesson in spiritual anatomy now enables us to appreciate and comprehend **the challenge of free choice**: will the heart sway to the evil inclination on the left and be governed by the influence of *nefesh* from the liver and the animal soul, thus gravitating downward toward evil, or sway to the right, to the upright spirit of *ruach* and the human soul while accepting the yoke of *neshama* in the brain and the influence of the Divine soul, thus gravitating upward toward good and righteousness? No other creation in the universe has this choice, for no other creation has a Divine soul, a human soul and an animal soul.

Neither an animal nor an angel has free choice for the animal has nothing but a basic animal soul and its accompanying instincts, which are not desires and aspirations. The animal does what it must do to survive; it might kill for food and fight when threatened, but it doesn't do willful harm. In that respect, when a human does evil by following the dictates of the animal soul, he or she is below the level of an animal.

On the other hand, an angel has nothing but a Divine soul and is therefore programmed to do good. It has no evil inclination or opposing spiritual force to overcome. In that respect, when a human overcomes formidable resistance to enable his or her Divine soul to prevail over their animal soul, they attain a higher spiritual level than the angels.

Residents of the Heart

Desire isn't the only resident of the heart. Emotions such as hate, love, sadness and depression are there also. Spiritually, **evil** – the influence of the animal soul - bends the heart out of shape and depresses it. **Good**, the influence of the Divine soul, straightens the heart and uplifts it. King David teaches that the "straight of heart are happy" (Psalm 97:11). Conversely, in the holy tongue of Torah, the word for a false idol – *etzev* – is the same word for sadness, showing us that sadness comes from the evil inclination's conquest of the heart.

We now arrive at a remarkable conclusion: **we have the free choice to gravitate toward happiness, by following the dictates of the Divine soul that uplifts us, or Heaven forbid, to gravitate toward sadness, by succumbing to the dictates of the animal soul that pulls us down.**

The objective of the evil inclination is to vanquish a person by inactivating the human and Divine souls. Since the animal soul in human beings and the evil inclination are perfectly synchronized, and the moment that the desires in the heart and the intellect in the brain become subservient to the body, one's so-called "intellect" is nothing other than a self-gratifying, bodily-oriented ideology.

To be exact, a person may think that his or her intellect prevails, causing influence to flow properly down to the heart and then to the body. Yet, if a person's intellect is based on human logic rather than Divine wisdom – emuna and the Torah – then it will be subservient to the bodily desires.

Attaining the Noble Flow

Top attain the noble flow, one must acquire Divine wisdom by learning Torah and strengthening emuna. This does not come easy! The body resists and the evil inclination puts up a tremendous fight. Without emuna, the body will be lax in learning Torah and performing its commandments, easily succumbing to temptation and wrongdoing.

Therefore, without internalizing the thirteen principles of emuna, the brain, blinded by the body's urges and the heart's desire to seek bodily amenities, will make its lust-and-body-friendly decisions. Without emuna, there cannot be free choice. The brain becomes an unprotected fortress, easily falling captive to the body.

Conclusion

The common denominator of our great spiritual leaders from our forefather Abraham, to Moses, to Rebbe Akiva, and down to such leaders of latter centuries such as the Chofetz Chaim is their noble, perfectly-ordered spiritual flow from top to bottom. This enabled them to function in an optimal manner even under extreme adversity.

Rebbe Shimon bar Yochai teaches that we are all capable of emulating our noble matriarchs and patriarchs when he says that we are all sons and daughters of nobility (tractate Shabbos 67a). Therefore, to make noble choices in life, we must do what our forefathers did and fill our brain with proper spiritual nutrition in order, thereby developing the highest possible potential of spiritual cognizance. This leads to upright choices and a gratifying life with heaven-on-earth inner peace. That is the benefit of learning, knowing and living the Eleventh Principle of Emuna and taking responsibility for everything we do.

The Twelfth Principle: Moshiach

Principle 12: I believe with complete belief in the coming of the Messiah, and even though he tarries, I will nonetheless await him every day, whenever he comes.

We believe that *Moshiach* (the Messiah) has not yet come, but we eagerly anticipate his arrival together with the advent of the Messianic era that includes the *Geula*, the full redemption of our people, the ingathering of the exiles to our holy homeland of Israel and the rebuilding of our Holy Temple in Jerusalem.

So much has been said and written about Moshiach and Geula throughout the years, not all of which is authoritative and in accordance with Torah and *mesorah*, genuine Jewish tradition. With that in mind, our belief in Moshiach is based on the teachings of the Rambam, who disperses the myths and clarifies the truth.

Belief in Moshiach

In his elaboration of the Mishna, the Rambam writes: "We are obliged to believe in the coming of Moshiach and not think that it will be delayed; that even though Moshiach tarries, we nonetheless await him. A person should not speculate about the time of his arrival, nor look for proofs in Torah that seemingly predict the time of his coming, for our sages say (Tractate Sanhedrin 96a), 'May the breathing of those who calculate the end cease.'" "The end" means the pre-Messasinic era and the beginning of the Messianic era.

Why would our gentle, peace-loving sages utter such a fierce curse against those who speculate about the date and time of Moshiach's arrival? I heard a wonderful answer from Rabbi Azriel Tauber osb"m, who himself was a Holocaust survivor. He explained, "The belief in Moshiach and Geula gave us the strength to endure such a purgatory as the Holocaust. But, if someone would have given a date, and Moshiach would not have arrived by then, we might have lost heart."

In light of Rabbi Tauber's explanation, we can understand how all the false messiahs in our history caused so much damage and breakdown of faith. Gullible people put all their hope in a deadline or a person, and when neither materialized, they lost faith. For that reason, a cynic once quipped that the tobacco companies finance false messiahs and messiah-date speculation, for when either proves false, many people begin smoking cigarettes on Shabbos, Heaven forbid...

The Rambam therefore stresses, "...even though Moshiach tarries, we nonetheless await him," any day he arrives. Our sages went to great lengths to prepare themselves for Moshiach and Geula.

Anticipation, not Speculation

One of the most important questions that the Heavenly Court asks a person immediately after he or she terminates their tour of duty in the physical world is, "Did you anticipate salvation?" (see tractate Shabbos 31a). Our sages elaborate that salvation is a package that includes Moshiach, Geula and the rebuilding of the Holy Temple in Jerusalem. As such, the anticipation of salvation is synonymous with the anticipation of Moshiach, for Moshiach is the catalyst that activates the process of salvation.

Moshiach and salvation are juxtaposed in the daily Amidah prayer, which we recite three times daily. In the *matzmiach keren yeshua* blessing we say, "Speedily cause the scion of David Your servant to flourish, and increase his power by Your salvation, for we hope for Your salvation all day and we anticipate salvation." The "scion of David" is Moshiach of course, and our double expression of hoping daily for salvation while constantly anticipating – when said with intent – enables each of us to answer the Heavenly Court, "Yes, I anticipated salvation, every single day and all day long."

We beg Hashem for Moshiach and the wonderful happenings that come with his arrival – redemption, ingathering of the exiles, the rebuilding of the Holy Temple in Jerusalem and the inundation of the world with the knowledge of Hashem and spiritual awareness.

We're far from finished in asking for Moshiach by way of the Amidah prayer alone. In Grace After Meals, *birkat hamazon,* we repeatedly ask for Moshiach and the rebuilding of Jerusalem. Every time we say the *Kaddish* prayer we say, *"b'agala u'bzman kariv"*, it should all come speedily and in our days. In the *Aleinu* prayer, also recited three times daily and four times on Shabbos, we beg Hashem to bring down the Divine Monarchy to this earth, and to wipe away all evil. Our liturgy is consequently geared to stimulate our eager anticipation of the "salvation package" that includes Moshiach, the building of the Holy Temple and the Geula, all of which mark the establishment of Hashem's reign on earth.

On Shabbos morning, we all cry out from the bottom of our hearts during the *Kedusha,* "When will You reign in Zion? Speedily in our days, shall You dwell among us forever!" With the spiritually-suffocating atmosphere of immorality, debauchery and agnosticism that characterizes modern society, we yearn for Moshiach just like we would yearn for fresh air in a heavily smoke-filled environment where a person could barely breathe. Moshiach's arrival marks the beginning of Hashem's reign on earth.

Our anticipation of Moshiach is so very important that the Gemara says anyone who doesn't believe in his coming is a heretic. The Rambam therefore stipulates that, "Anyone who does not believe in him or one who does not anticipate his coming not only denies the Prophets, but also the Torah and Moses our Teacher" (Hilchot Melachim 11:1).

Our great spiritual leaders anticipated Moshiach and Geula with all their hearts, and practically as well. The Chofetz Chaim established a special rabbinical seminary for learning all the laws that apply to the Holy Temple and Divine service there, laws which few are familiar with today on an in-depth basis. What's more, the Chofetz Chaim had a special festive coat that he planned to wear when he greeted Moshiach, and he would don it from time to time in anticipation.

Anticipation is not speculation and date-guessing. The Rambam reiterates the Gemara's curse against those who speculate on the time of Moshiach's arrival (Hilchot Melachim 12:2). Speculation is potentially devastating, for when it fails to materialize, many of those who had their hopes held high fall to disappointment and despair at the expense of whatever level of emuna they might have had.

Whereas speculation is a blemish in simple emuna, anticipation is not. "Even though he tarries, I'll nonetheless await him every day, whenever he may come;" this is the purest declaration of true emuna.

Who is Moshiach?

The Rambam stresses that Moshiach is a human being like everyone else and writes, "Don't think that King Moshiach must perform miracles and wonders and unprecedented actions in the world or revive the dead and so forth" (Hilchos Melachim 11:3). The Rambam hereby shows the stark contrast of our concept of Moshiach and other religions' idea of messiah.

Once the Rambam stipulates that Moshiach need not be a miracle worker, he differentiates between the genuine Moshiach and the false messiah (ibid, 4): "If King Moshiach will arise from the descendants of the House of David and immerses himself in Torah and in mitzvah observance like his forefather David, both written Torah and Oral Torah, and he leads all of Israel to lead lives of Torah and to strengthen themselves in every detail of observance, and he fights the battles of Hashem, then he can be *regarded to be* Moshiach. If he has done all this and has succeeded, and in addition has rebuilt the Temple in its proper place and has gathered in the exiles, then he is *certainly* Moshiach."

Let's pay close attention to the Rambam's differentiation between "regarded to be" Moshiach and "certainly" Moshiach and compare between the two:

Regarded to be Moshiach

1. Descendant of David;

2. Immersed in Torah and mitzvah observance;

3. Leads all of Israel to lead lives of Torah – not just a small group but everyone, secular and religious, all ethnic groups, with no exception;

4. He fights all those who rise up against Hashem and His Torah.

If he fulfills the above four conditions, totally and not partially, we are obliged to regard him as Moshiach.

Certainly Moshiach

1. He defeats the enemies of Hashem and His Torah;

2. He builds the Holy Temple in its proper place in Jerusalem;

3. He gathers the exiles from the four corners of the earth to our holy homeland in the Land of Israel.

If he also fulfills the above three conditions, then he is certainly Moshiach.

Clearly, no one in history since King David has come close to fulfilling the prerequisites of "regarded to be Moshiach", much less "certainly Moshiach.

Life in the Era of Moshiach

After the Rambam describes the nature of Moshiach, he writes about what life in the era of Moshiach will be like (ibid, Ch.12): "Don't think that the natural course of the world will be altered [during the time of Moshiach] but nature shall continue to run its course." In other words, things as they are now will not change. A person will still make pay monthly mortgage and electric bills. Moshiach won't pay off people's credit card or dental bills. There will still be rich people and poor people, weak and strong.

What, then, will be different once Moshiach comes?

The monarchy will return to the House of David. The world will fill with knowledge of the Almighty. Earning an income will be much easier for those who devote their lives to Divine service. The big difference between the Messianic Era and now is that once Moshiach comes, it will be much easier to learn Torah and to observe the mitzvoth. This is all geared to prepare the world for its ultimate rectification.

Now is the Time

There's a big disadvantage of the Messianic Era as opposed to now, when we still await Moshiach despite pandemics and existential threats from our enemies. The value of our emuna and teshuva will be much less, since the whole world will see the Hashem is One and His Name is One. Only an imbecile will transgress Hashem's laws and that will be tantamount to suicide. This is what our sages described as, "The Needless Days, when there is no reward and no punishment" (Vayikra Raba 18:1). Therefore, now is the time to reap the full benefits of strengthening emuna and purifying ourselves in teshuva.

Why then do we yearn for Moshiach?

There is no greater sublime pleasure anywhere than getting to know Hashem and getting close to Him. The days of Moshiach will bring mankind to a spiritual level beyond what we can fathom today, for on that day, "…thus speaks Hashem, 'I will put My Torah in their midst and will write it on their hearts; and I will be their God, and they shall be My people…for they shall all know Me'" (Jeremiah 31:32-33). That is the joyous day that we all anticipate, speedily and in our days, amen!

The Thirteenth Principle: Resurrection

Principle 13: I believe with complete belief that there will be a resurrection of the dead at the prescribed time that the Creator wills, blessed be His Name and may He be exalted forever and ever.

We believe that death as we know it today is a passing stage and not terminal, for we believe in the resurrection of the dead.

The Thirteenth Principle is very important that we allude to it six times in the initial three-benediction section of the Amidah prayer, which we recite every single day, weekdays, Sabbath and festivals:

1. "You are forever mighty, my Lord; You resurrect the dead."

2. "He sustains the living with loving kindness, resurrects the dead with great mercy."

3. "[He] fulfills His promise to those who slumber in the dust."

4. "King Who brings death and restores life;"

5. "You are trustworthy to revive the dead."

6. "Blessed are You Hashem, Who revives the dead."

Halacha places such critical importance on the initial three-benediction section of the Amidah prayer that one may neither add nor detract a single word, whereas in the middle benedictions of the Amidah, one may (see Shulchan Aruch, Orach Chaim, 112:1). In his elaboration of this law, the Chafetz Chaim explains that the initial three benedictions are like a servant praising his master whereas the later benedictions are like a servant requesting his needs from his master (ibid, Mishna Brura, 1.a).

In light of the Chafetz Chaim's above teaching, we must ask ourselves: of the infinite praises that the Creator deserves, why did the Men of the Great Assembly[4] put such an emphasis on the resurrection of the dead, which we mention not once, but six times?

---

[4] "Anshei Knesses Hagdolah," Ezra and his court who codified our liturgy (see Meiri on Megilla 17a)

The Greatest Consolation

Rebbe Shlomo HaCohen Rabinowitz of Radomsk (1801-1866) reminds us (see Tiferes Shlomo, Chayei Sarah) that the blessing of reviving the dead was first codified by our forefather Isaac, for when his father Abraham bound him to the altar in the *Akeda*[5], and he was about to be slaughtered, his soul left his body. Yet when the angel stopped Abraham from slaughtering him, Isaac's soul returned to him. From this, Isaac knew that Hashem revives the dead.

The "Tiferes Shlomo" continues to describe Isaac's anguish when his father Abraham died. All the generations from Adam to Abraham were created solely for the purpose of bringing Abraham into the world. Abraham was the first monotheist. His knowledge of Hashem was so prodigious that he knew and practiced all of Torah. He knew the secrets of creation as well as we see in his monumental *Sefer Hayetzira*, the first Kabbalistic book. Isaac had no one else to learn from; his father was a giant of an individual and one of a kind for

---

[5] Literally "binding," Abraham's tenth test of faith, when Hashem commands Abraham to bind his son Isaac to the altar as a sacrificial offering (see Genesis 22: 1-19).

posterity. Abraham's departure from the physical world devastated his son Isaac.

Isaac could find no consolation, says the "Tiferes Shlomo", until he remembered his own blessing, "Blessed are You Hashem, Who revives the dead."

Our sages teach that while Abraham's leading trait was the love of Hashem, Isaac's was the fear of Hashem. Logically, the *Akeda* was more of a test of Abraham's faith than of Isaac's: how could Abraham, the pillar of love and compassion, slaughter his son on the altar. Yet Isaac, the architype of God-fearing individuals, would be willing at any moment to be sacrificed for Hashem. Little did Isaac realize at the time, according to the Tiferes Shlomo's teachings, that his near-death experience (NDE), where he tangibly tasted death as his soul left his body, would be his greatest consolation.

Isaac, in his prodigious spirit of holiness, came to the realization that this physical life as we know it is temporary. He wasn't the same after the *Akeda* as he was before. So too, Hashem will revive the dead and they too won't be the same, but on a much higher level of spiritual awareness. The realization that his father Abraham would some day return on a yet loftier level than his first 175 years on earth, filled Isaac with immense joy – this was his greatest consolation at the loss of his father.

As a nation, our suffering ever since the wicked King Nimrod pursued and persecuted Abraham has been unprecedented. Exile, suffering, torture, occupation, destruction, Crusades, Inquisition, pogroms and Holocaust are all key words in our history. If that's not enough, even this generation has been subject to pandemics, terminal diseases and sudden inexplicable tragedies like crib deaths and young people dying suddenly.

If I'm not mistaken, this is the reason the Men of the Great Assembly put such a huge emphasis on the resurrection of the dead, which we mention not once, but six times in our liturgy's most important prayer, the first three benedictions of the Amidah. Ezra, Nechemiah, Mordechai, Daniel, Haggai and Zachariah of the Great Assembly were prophets as well. They knew that the Jewish People would need massive daily reinforcement of emuna and consolation in order to weather such trying times without suffering a breakdown of faith. Therefore, they remind us over and over that Hashem will – without the slightest doubt – revive the dead. They renew Isaac's benediction and codify, "Blessed are You Hashem, Who revives the dead." The benediction in writing uses the ineffable Name; orally, we say Hashem's Name of "our Lord", *A'donoi*. Were it not absolutely true with an iota of a doubt, the Third of the Ten Commandments would not allow us to make such a blessing, for it would be taking Hashem's Name in vain, Heaven forbid.

How could anyone fathom that the holy Men of the Great Assembly, themselves prophets such as Ezra, Daniel and Mordechai, would mislead generations for the next 24 centuries and cause them to violate the Ten Commandments multiple times a day? Nothing could be a greater absurdity! If they codified a benediction for the resurrection of the dead, we can be a million-percent sure that it will be!

The Promise

The Men of the Great Assembly tell Hashem and us why they can so confidently codify the *Mechaye HaMesim* (resurrection of the dead) benediction with Hashem's holy Name in our liturgy. A promise precedes the benediction: "You are trustworthy to revive the dead." Explains the Meiri (Discourse on Teshuva, Meshiv Nefesh, Ch. 8) that Hashem's trustworthiness is His reliability in fulfilling his promise. Most noteworthy is that the Hebrew word for "trustworthy", which is synonymous to "faithful", is *ne'eman*, a derivative of the word *emuna*. Hashem's promises of redemption and resurrection are so trustworthy that we believe in them without the slightest doubt.

This promise, in itself, is the greatest consolation for anyone who has ever lost a loved one. Like money in the bank, it's a promissory note from Hashem that's cosigned by the holy Men of the Great Assembly.

Hashem declares, "See now that I, I am He, and there is no god with Me; I cause death and I shall revive" (Deuteronomy 32:39). Asks Rabbenu Bachiya in his elaboration of this passage why Hashem repeats "I" where once would seemingly suffice. There's a double reason: first, just as Hashem knows about our current exile and Diaspora, He knows about our imminent redemption. Second, just as Hashem brings death, He will surely revive the dead. This Torah promise, even more than a promise but a statement of fact, is repeated by the prophet: "Hashem causes death and resurrects; He lowers one to the grave, then raises him up" (Samuel I, 2:6).

Revival of Every Last Particle

After death and burial, the body undergoes a natural process of decomposition, as the Torah says, "For you are dust and you shall return to dust" (Genesis 3:19). Yet, many times in history, a cemetery is plowed up into a potato field and the ashes of the deceased are scattered in the four winds. What happens then? Even worse, what becomes of a deceased person who died at sea and whose body is thrown overboard rather than being properly buried? And yet worse than that is the fate of the Holocaust martyrs who were burned to ash in the crematoriums. What about them?

I often asked myself the above questions, especially in regard to all the Holocaust martyrs in our family. Rabbi Shimon Agasi (1852-1914), one of Baghdad's renowned scholars and Kabbalists from the generation of the Ben Ish Chai, wrote a book entitled *Yesodai HaTorah*, "The Foundations of Torah," which I was first introduced to through the writings of Rabbi Azriel Tauber osb"m.

Citing the ninth chapter of Tractate Kela'im in the Yerushalmi Talmud, Rabbi Agasi writes that when resurrecting the dead, Hashem will return every particle, no matter where it is scattered, to its rightful body. Similar concepts are expressed in the writings of the holy Shl"a and the Mahara'l of Prague. Nothing shall be lost. This too is a wonderful consolation for all of us.

Giving Birth in the Inferno

Let's conclude this chapter on Principle Thirteen with a poignant story about a courageous woman's emuna in the revival of the dead.

Although Rabbi Azriel Tauber was born shortly before the Holocaust, his four brothers and sisters were born during the years 1940-1944, in the midst of the Nazi inferno. Miraculously, the first three of the four were saved. But, when his mother was expecting the fourth, she was sent to Auschwitz, where she became a guinea pig for the sadistic Nazi doctors' experiments under the direction of the arch-murderer Mengele. As she gave birth, the Nazis murdered the baby, a precious little girl who became a martyr in her first moment outside the womb. Yet, as the baby's grueling death satisfied the sadistic Nazis, Rabbi Tauber's mother was spared. After the war, she gave birth to five more children.

At one point after the war, Rabbi Tauber asked his mother: "Mama, when you became pregnant during the Holocaust and gave birth, did you ever think that your children would survive?"

His mother answered, "My son, I knew that I wasn't better than anyone else. Sure, I feared for my life and for the lives of my children. Nevertheless, I gave birth to them with no regrets. After all, we believe in revival of the dead. According to the principles of our faith, there is no such thing as losing children for posterity. Every child I brought into the world is eternal, and despite the Nazis, may their name be obliterated, our people are eternal."

Nothing like our belief in the revival of the dead is so encouraging and empowering, giving us the strength to continue on despite the worst hardships, for we can look forward to the day when Hashem will declare, "Awaken and sing, you who dwell in the dust" (Isaiah 26:19), fulfilling His promises of bringing us Moshiach, ingathering the exiles, reviving the dead, and rebuilding our

Holy Temple in Jerusalem, speedily and in our days, amen!

Completed by the grace of Hashem here in the Holy Land of Israel, Adar, 5781

More Titles by Rabbi Lazer Brody Available on Amazon

3 Words of Emuna

"**Three Words of Emuna**" is a practical guide to the three most important words in the Torah, *Ein Od Milvado*, and their amazing power in freeing a person from anxiety and negative emotions. In unprecedented clarity, Rabbi Brody explains the three fundamental principles of **emuna** as well, the basis of pure and complete faith and key to inner peace and a happy life.

The Path to Your Peak

We all have the potential of reaching the top. People fail to reach their own special peak because of two main reasons: first, they don't properly utilize and take advantage of their personal potential. Second, they don't have a plan. To do anything successfully, whether it's becoming a champion athlete, a successful businessperson, an honor student, an efficient homemaker or anything else you desire to do, you need a plan. With that in mind, this book will provide you with a tailor-made, practical plan for success that you can readily implement.

Old Isaac's Trail to Tranquility

Old Isaac is an allegorical innkeeper whose coarse exterior hides his amazing wisdom and his gentle, understanding and very loving nature. He leads his guests – the readers of this book – along a very beautiful and educational trail that leads to an anger-free life of satisfaction, genuine happiness and inner peace.

Chassidic Pearls

This book is designed to make the family's festive Shabbat meal an unforgettable experience that every member of the family eagerly anticipates all week long. **Chassidic Pearls** is a collection of Rabbi Lazer Brody's original parables that elaborate on the weekly Torah portions with a distinct Chassidic flavor. Each weekly "pearl" enables everyone to enjoy and appreciate the wisdom of Torah on their own individual level while warming the hearts of the entire family.

Printed in Great Britain
by Amazon